Life is Funny

129 random, ridiculous, and sometimes
inappropriate observations about life, people, and
the stupid situations we find ourselves in
on a daily basis

seven Munson

Published by So Unserious
Printed in the United States of America
ISBN 978-0-578-42666-2

Table of Contents

Introduction 1

Casinos 3

The Mustache 4

Midgets 5

Monkeys 6

Oranges 8

The Airport 10

Halloween 12

I Could Care Less 14

TV Adds 10 Pounds 15

TV Phone Numbers 16

People Who Drive Without Lights 17

Family Feud Hosts 18

Zack Morris Timeout 20

Birthday Wishes 21

Sandwiches 22

Bathroom Things 24

Movie Previews 28

People Who Don't Wear Seatbelts 30

Dudes Who Drive Convertibles 32

Non-Handicapped Assholes Who Use the
Handicap Tag on Their Car...33

Stage Dancers for Pop Stars...34

People Who Fight 35

People Who Set Their Clocks Ahead So They
Aren't Late...36

Popular Song Lyrics...37

Plane Rules 38

Jennifer Aniston 41

Trying Someone Else's Food...42

Bill, Not Check...44

Restaurant Specials...46

"A" As In 47

Kiss..48

Animal Siblings..49

Clean, Dirty Words 50

Jockeys 52

Adults Riding in Cars 53

Closed Captioning...54

Albert Pujols 55

Car Dealership Flags...56

Bedding...57

Poor Investments 58

Hibernation 60

Handicap Stall 62

Holding Doors 64

Commence 66

Mount Rushmore 68

Meeting People 69

Toothpaste 71

The National Debt 73

New Things 74

Stuff That's Given Away 76

Rest Stops 77

Double Cheek Greeting 78

Fancy Silverware 79

Speeding 80

Office Lights 82

Pluto 83

Lefties 84

Work Clothes 85

Dance Dance Revolution 86

Unneeded Jobs 87

Dropped Calls 88

Virginity Rules 89

Chinese Envy 90

Building Things 91

Bidets 92

People Who Look Back 94

Elevators 95

Over 21 to Drink 96

Close Families 97

Peeing in Urinals 99

Passing on the Message 100

Honorary Degrees 101

Nose Maintenance 103

Children's Author 104

Sammy the Snail Slithers South 105

Pirates 123

The Mirror Look 124

A Flurry of Questions 125

Chickenpox 130

Acting 132

Ratios 133

Smackers 134

The Night Shower 135

Saying You Know What a Person Is Talking
About When You Have No Idea 136

The Corporate World 137

Skipped Poops 140

The Best Music Video of All Time 141

Talking While Calling Someone 142

Graffiti 143

Entering a Vehicle 144

People Don't Work 145

Makeup 146

Yanking Your Yo-Yo 147

NASA 149

Art 151

Rich People 152

Gift Cards 154

Rioting 155

The Itch 156

Thunderstorms 157

Handkerchiefs 158

The Mute Button 159

Richard 160

Amish 161

Warehouses 163

Nincumpoop 164

Vomiting 165

Pronunciation 166

The Shirt Neck 167

Astronaut Food 168

The Butt Slap 169

Divas 170

Leftovers 172

Who Will Talk Next 174

Fake Names 176

Magicians 177

Stars and Oceans 179

Bed Rest 180

Mall Kiosks 181

Tater Tots 182

Sharting 183

The 10 185

Kids Who Wear T-Shirts in the Pool 186

Ranch 187

Rubbernecking 189

Low Pressure Water Fountains 191

Cows 192

Fetishes 194

Seasonal Things 195

Going Potty Outside the Potty 198

Closing Thoughts 201

About the Author 202

Introduction

Well hello there. It's very nice to meet you. I can't see you, but if you bought this book you're probably pretty attractive, so congratulations. Someday you can let me know how it feels.

First and foremost, I want you to rest assured knowing that every penny of profit from this book will go to charity—charities that support puppy mills and chicken farms. Purebreds are way too expensive and the price of individually wrapped chicken breast is outrageous. I'm a fan of anything that drives these costs down.

Throughout the epic journey you're about to embark on, there's a good chance you'll have a number of questions along the way. Challenge yourself. Ask yourself why. Look deeper. Don't settle.

All of the following characters, settings, plots, stories, and climaxes are real. There have been no fabrications. I'm just a really good climaxer.

You'll feel many things throughout this magical journey. Sometimes you'll agree with me. Sometimes you'll disagree with me. Sometimes you'll feel awkward. But there will also be times when you'll feel like a cumulous cloud floating innocently amongst a sun-drenched ocean blue sky. In these cases, you'll feel swell.

Ultimately and hopefully, you'll be able to forget about the seriousness of everyday life. Maybe you'll even touch yourself.

In any case, I hope you enjoy. This is meant to be enjoyed. That's all.

So, welcome to the book. I apologize in advance.

Casinos

I'm all for gambling, but sometimes I can't stand going into a casino. After forking over the $8 surcharge to withdraw five Benjamin Franklins, the bankruptcy clock immediately starts ticking. Whether it happens right off the bat as the ball trickles to a stop on red, or when you double up only to lose it later after a second throw in the back room of a strip club. It doesn't really matter. However you slice it, you're going down.

Why do dudes feel obligated to wear their Sunday best to the casino? I understand wanting to get it in, but why would anyone voluntarily wear a suit on the weekend? Hot girls in a casino want nothing to do with you unless you're willing to throw down 500 bucks for an HJ at the closest Rodeway Inn.

Always prioritize comfort over beauty. And always be sure to rub one out before you hit the blackjack table. It's a much smoother conversation with the wife when you can blame a $500 loss on the cards, instead of some paraplegic's left hand.

The Mustache

Ahhh, the age-old question: When is it socially acceptable for a man to grow and wear a mustache for an extended period of time?

Think about it. Think about the people you know who have one. It really is one of the hardest questions to answer. At what point can you take someone seriously enough to not laugh?

The period between pre-mustache and mustache is almost as awkward as having one in the first place. I'm familiar with the beard-growing strategy where you grow everything out and shave the surrounding areas when it's ready; but even then, there will always be a point in the journey when the hair above your lip looks like it was dipped in a tub of ground up acorns and pig feces. As for the acceptable age to wear poop-smashed nuts on your face, I say at least 45.

Personally, I'm still waiting for my facial hair to fill in, but I tried to grow one in college once. It was pretty ironic. I looked like a 13-year-old pedophile.

Midgets

Midgets are mesmerizing. My guess is the two greatest advantages of being a midget are the fact that your pants never touch the bathroom floor if you're pooping and being able to wash a considerable amount of clothes per load every time you do laundry.

Have you ever seen a 17-year-old midget? No chance. They don't exist. Every midget is 40. How do they get to this age and where do they go after?

Monkeys

Everyone knows monkeys are awesome. They throw their own poop, eat bananas like it's nobody's business, hold stuff in their feet, brush their teeth, go on piggyback rides, and are always up for a good time. There are far too many things you can do in the presence of a monkey.

One of my goals in life is to own one. I'm not sure whether or not it'll be for an extended period of time, but I do know that at some point on my journey, owning a monkey will be necessary.

My dream monkey day would most likely go as follows:

I'd pick Ned up from preschool around 12:30. Yes, an uneducated monkey is a glorious time, but imagine how much cooler he'd be if he could stack blocks and paint with watercolors. After some breakfast for lunch at IHOP, we'd carelessly cruise around in my Ford Econoline cargo van. Ned would be on top, of course. Surf's up. Ever since my first screening of Teen Wolf, I've dreamed of the day when a monkey would turn miraculous flips on the roof of my creepy windowless van.

Once low tide rolled in and the waves settled down, I'd give him countless behind-the-back high-fives, and we'd polish off the day with a cold one. If Ned's drinking, he's shotgunning. I'd reach for my keys. Ned would stop me. He'd grab both cans and simultaneously Teen Wolf beer-bite 'em. A perfect cut. Best beer of my life.

Oranges

Why on earth is it so hard to peel an orange?

Million-dollar idea. Someone come up with a tool that automatically peels it for you. There's got to be some technology out there that can do this sort of thing. Put your orange in a device, and bam, it comes out skinless and juicy. I mean, if we could fake a moon landing…

A few days ago, I was standing over the garbage can, frustrated as usual. Ideally, you have to break the skin perfectly. If you don't, you end up leaving too much of that white crap on the outside. I didn't go deep enough. The entire peel was over from there.

For whatever reason, peeling a clementine is like opening an Easter egg. It's ridiculously easy. But you're setting yourself up to fail when you upgrade to a navel. They're impossible to peel and are easily one of the most overrated fruits. Between the skin, excess white stuff, and pointless strings, there's way too much going on. And if there are seeds inside, forget about it. I always associate peeling a hefty navel with performing cunnilingus. In the end it usually works out in your favor, but those five minutes of hell always make you second guess the next go around.

There's no doubt an orange tastes fantastic though. So like I said, if someone makes something that peels it right and splits it up for you, they're going to bank. Ten bucks, I'd buy one.

Or better yet, I could break the restraining order, move back in with Mom, and make her peel all of my oranges for me again.

The Airport

There's nothing like a trip to the airport. Mobile ticketing has sped up a previously painful process, but there are still quite a few things throughout this experience that are excruciatingly enjoyable.

The security checkpoint is awesome. Here, we wait in line for 15 minutes to take our clothes off. Unless you're rocking Umbros, you're walking up to bat with a belt on. Whether you forget to take it off the first time through, or if you're a usual, no matter what, that belt's coming off. And when it does, hold on tight.

I usually step into the scanner, raise my arms, and wait ten minutes for my stuff because the idiot in front of me just realized packing a Costco-sized body wash is frowned upon.

Once my stuff shows up, I pull it to the side and stand there like an asshole, trying to find the same belt latch I went in with. It never happens though. I always plug in way too early and end up having to re-adjust 125 yards down the line in front of the Applebee's To Go. But before I know it, my pants are around my ankles and my tip's flapping in the wind. I've never owned a pair of boxers with a button in my entire life. Shame on me because it's a very underwhelming sight. People who catch a glimpse must assume I'm transitioning or something.

There's nothing wrong with being a grower not a shower.

Halloween

Halloween has a lot of things going for it. It can easily be broken down in two completely different types of celebrations: kid Halloween and college Halloween. College Halloween isn't even fair, so don't get me started.

As a kid, it doesn't get much better than grabbing your pillowcase and throwing on a bloody mask. You walk out the door, go house-to-house, ring a bell, and are promptly rewarded with a candy bar. Whoever created this "holiday" is a genius.

Although it's clearly awesome, there are some bullshit things about Halloween. The people who don't participate whatsoever are complete scumbags. Really? You can't muster up a few fun size Snickers bars, answer your door to the looks of joyous children, and take the hit? Sorry to interrupt you from doing nothing, but come on. We know you're home. Just because you turn your outside light off doesn't mean we can't see you. If you're willing to go through that sort of effort to disappoint a child, then you're just a huge dick.

On the flip side, there are the people who at least participate, but are some of the worst "treaters" you could ever imagine. It always astonishes me that year after year, people actually think to themselves, "Hey, this will be great, the kids will love these," while ravaging through their drawers the day of, pulling out pennies, rabbit feet, and sugar packets. Yes, rabbit feet and sugar packets. I've been a lucky recipient of these a few times over the years. At least throw a little coke in the packets. Let the kids live a little.

But seriously, college Halloween. Oh, the girls.

I Could Care Less

So simple, yet very tough for many people to grasp. People swear they are portraying how little they care about something, but they omit one of the most important contractions in the English language.

"I could care less about Hitler." See, now you made yourself look like a giant dick because you stated you have some level of care for Hitler.

You *couldn't* care less about Hitler. You could *not*.

TV Adds 10 Pounds

Where? Why? No, it doesn't. Mr. Belding is just that fat now.

TV Phone Numbers

Why was "555" officially dubbed as the fake area code that's used in every old school TV show or movie? I thought Hollywood was a little more creative than this. I love when shows use "KL5" as a cover-up, like it's a completely different number people don't even know about yet. A lot of folks, including myself, are stupid, but seriously, mix it up a bit.

Louisiana ditched their 666 area code for religious concerns. According to Wikipedia, it's the number of the beast. Perfect for Hollywood. Although, it'll probably have to involuntarily watch a fat dude jerk off before getting the job.

People Who Drive Without Lights

I'm sure you regularly spot cars well into the night coming right at you with no lights on. And I'm not talking about those one-on, one-off guys. I'm talking none. Every time I wonder, "How is this possibly happening? How has this person traveled this far and failed to realize they're not being guided by any light?"

I see this way more than I should when I'm coming home from work. I understand forgetting at first after pulling out of the driveway, but on a highway? Maybe these people are hardcore environmentalists. I have no clue how lights impact your car's battery life or gas intake, but maybe this is top of mind for these people. Maybe they're cheap. Maybe they like to steal light from other cars. Maybe they have a lot of faith in the streetlights that line the road every quarter mile. Or maybe, and most likely, they're idiots.

From here on out, just run right into them. You're not at fault. You'll get a sweet insurance payout to upgrade your car and, if you're lucky, the other driver will be stuck in traffic school with Lindsay Lohan for the next 6 months. I think she's still there.

Family Feud Hosts

Richard Dawson (1976-1985, 1994–1995)

Ray Combs (1988–1994)

Louie Anderson (1999–2002)

Richard Karn (Borland) (2002–2006)

John O'Hurley (Peterman) (2006–2010)

Steve Harvey (2010-Present)

These were the legends. Well, some were at least. There always seemed to be a ton of controversy surrounding *Family Feud* hosts. It's probably because every host thought it was oddly necessary to grab/caress/kiss/pet/tickle/stroke each and every female contestant on the show. Even today, you can catch reruns from old school shows with Dawson, or new school shows with Borland or Peterman, and see how uncomfortable the exchanges between the host and contestants are.

This icky behavior is always most evident during the fast money round. The host will become far too friendly with the woman who's just trying to see whether or not her team mustered up enough points to take down the

20 grand. I recently watched a clip where Dawson went straight mouth-on-mouth with a girl after she sealed up the "W" for her fam.

She had braces.

Dawson definitely wins the douchiest host award.

Zack Morris Timeout

For all the religious *Saved by the Bell* watchers out there, we all know that in crucial situations, Zack Morris is somehow capable of stopping time. Zack simply has to make a "T" with his hands and say "Time Out" to the camera. During timeout, Zack's in the zone. This gives him six additional seconds to figure out the best solution to any given problem. These crucial seconds account for some of the best moments in all of television history.

My personal favorite is when Zack used this extraordinary power to dodge Slater's punch. Slater punched Mr. Belding in the face instead. Belding sucked, so this was okay with me, but if Slater had connected, I'm not sure if Zack would've lived—or more importantly, if there would've ever been a "Wedding in Las Vegas" four-episode series where Zack tied the knot with Kelly. Thank god he called time out.

Does he run out of these? Do they get replenished after a certain amount of time? Can he ever not be granted timeout? These questions keep me up at night.

Birthday Wishes

Dude, what the hell? What am I doing wrong? I'm officially 0 for 23 now. I don't think I knew what was going on the first four years of my life, but ever since I was five, I haven't come remotely close to having a birthday wish granted. It's not like I'm wishing for an extra penis or the ability to use the force. We're talking puppies, vacations, and snowstorms.

I'm a February birthday, so there were some occasions when I'd ask Old Man Winter to dump a few inches on our town for a school closing. I got nothing. Sunny and 45. Not even a chance of ice.

Lesson learned. Ignore this ridiculous superstition and never make a wish again. I just have to live with the fact that I'll never share a Niagara Falls barrel dive with Michael Bolton.

Sandwiches

Everyone loves a good sandwich. Not like you care, but my favorite's an Italian sub with lettuce, tomatoes, a few onions, oil, vinegar, salt, and pepper. Throw that on a soft Italian roll and I'm a happy camper.

Eating a sandwich is simple. In all situations, there are two crucial steps that should be taken before any sandwich is enjoyed. The first is meat distribution. It's imperative you know how to properly allocate meat. Depending on the creator, there may or may not be necessary pre-bite adjustments to evenly distribute the meats and condiments throughout the bread. The uneven sub is a nightmare, so make sure you get in there early and clean up the mess. Once you're satisfied with your pre-bite situation, dig in. However, dig in carefully. This is where it gets fun.

The second critical step to eating any good sandwich is first bite technique. The first bite is a science. It should set up the remaining 10-15 bites perfectly. Rotate the sandwich around three or four times to identify the optimal starting point. Each and every bite should contain the same layering of meat, lettuce, and sauce. If you're multiple bites deep before hitting a condiment, there's a serious problem. No sandwich deserves to be made that way.

Next time you're out, watch someone sit down with a sandwich. You'll be able to quickly identify the people who know what they're doing. Some people spin, but more should. There are still novices out there who throw themselves in no man's land immediately following their first bite.

Take your time. Consider your options. Trust yourself.

Bathroom Things

Why do people who design bathrooms omit the most vital part of lavatory construction? It's a very simple ask. Is the TP in a convenient enough place to be easily seen and grabbed by the pooper?

Be it at a restaurant, bar, office, or a friend's house, I constantly find myself reaching around in unfamiliar territory. The TP always seems to be in a peculiar position. Sometimes it's almost behind the toilet completely, creating a reach-around scenario. Sometimes it's around the corner, creating a cheek-off-the-seat scenario. And sometimes it's straight ahead of you ... but three feet ahead of you, creating a poop-drag-onto-the-front-rim-and-possibly-your-pants scenario. These are all scenarios I no longer want any part of. New rule: either all future toilets should have TP attached to them, or all TP holders should be placed in plain sight—no peripheral TP allowed—at no more than a foot from the pooper. This would not only make the cleanup smoother, but it would dramatically reduce your chances of rim poop.

During work the other day, I walked up to one of three

vacant urinals and naturally chose the one on the left, leaving the middle and right urinals open. Moments later, another dude walked in and, without hesitation, settled in right next to me, leaving the third and last urinal, all the way to the right, completely open. This is not cool, normal, or in any way acceptable in a male bathroom. At that point, I blacked out and don't know if I shook my little guy clean or washed my hands. I was really thrown off. What could possibly be going through someone's head to actually think, "Hmm, this seems like the most appropriate urinal for me to relieve myself. This won't be weird at all."

It's very awkward when you see a guy you work with all the time come out of a stall, say hi to you, and walk straight out without even looking at the sink. Everything from that point on is a little tainted. This does raise a question I've contemplated for years. After stocking the pond, have you ever felt so confident that you got up and walked away? I can't do it. I've thought about it a few times because by now you almost always know for sure what a ghost feels like, but I can't bring myself to that point. I'll never have that much confidence in myself. I can never go without a security wipe.

If you have, bravo, you're a fucking rock star.

Ass sneezing in general has caused a significant amount of awkward moments between people all over the world. If we all share one thing, it's what goes on behind closed doors. We poop, and usually, it stinks. Bathroom placement plays a huge factor in the aftermath of a poop. Some are tucked away in the basement, and some are two steps from the kitchen table.

I was at my buddy's house once and had to use his horribly placed bathroom. After an enormous Italian feast, I got one of those, "Wow, I just ate a boatload of food and it has absolutely nowhere to go because my body hasn't discharged the previous meal yet" types of poop cravings. And believe me, these come on quick and action needs to be taken immediately. I politely excused myself from the table and scooted off to the bathroom, which was four feet from where everyone was sitting. I knew right off the bat it was going to be a closed-door exit. I had a clinger that I couldn't shake loose for the life of me. I finally cleaned up, washed up, and opened every cabinet looking for the "spray." Nothing. Not good. I walked out and sat down. My buddy's grandma got up, walked in right after me, turned around, and literally said, "I guess I'll use the one upstairs."

A few bathroom situations to go out on:

- Have you ever battled a slice of mud pie for so long that a second round of pee came out?

- Ever run out of TP ... and tissues? What do you do? Shower curtain? Towel? Hand?

- Walking into the bathroom after your girlfriend of three months just tore it up like it was her job. Big win. Who doesn't like anal if it's within an hour of defecation? No need for lube.

Movie Previews

I absolutely love going to the movies. Nothing's better than posting up in front of an incredibly oversized screen with a bucket of popcorn and a tub of soda. Why do movie theaters size everything like they're a duty-free shop in an airport? Two gallons of soda? Sure, why not.

Why has only one person been allowed to do the preview voice for movies? This deep, thunderous, overly excited tone can make anything from Stuart Little to Honey sound like the best movie ever made. I know it's crazy, but why not have someone else do the voiceover for a change? This level of excitement is flat out unnecessary for a lot of previews. Unfortunately, not every movie is Die Hard.

I'm pretty sure the voiceover job req hasn't been modified since the Chaplin era because no one's in a rush to throw a woman behind the mic. Have you ever heard a female do a movie preview? I didn't think so. I even went back and YouTube'd *The Notebook* trailer just to make sure. It's not that I care about women having the same opportunities as men, but come on, that's Marketing 101. Take any chick flick, have anyone but Miley Cyrus do the voiceover, and *bam*, you got a gal blockbuster on your hands. I'm sure that was the only thing separating Honey from Oscar gold.

People Who Don't Wear Seatbelts

I'll never understand this for as long as I live—or don't live if I'm a moron like a lot of these people. For some reason, there's a stretch of time while growing up where the kids who don't wear seatbelts are the "cool kids." How does something like this gain traction? Why would you believe someone if they said, "Hey, you know what would make you way cooler? If you stop wearing a seatbelt while riding in a high-speed vehicle."

The way we act when we're riding with someone we've never met before is ludicrous. We get into the Uber or bus and don't even think about putting our seatbelt on. And if you're packing three in the back, forget about it. Human bodies instantly become seatbelts. It's only a matter of time before one of the jackasses you're with says something like, "No reason to put this on. There's no way any of us are moving back here."

I guess we're OK with trusting our lives to an extraordinarily awful driver while making the conscious decision to opt out of the seatbelt = safety concept. Why would the cabbie care if he dies? Leaving behind a 13 square foot apartment and four or five unpaid cable bills doesn't sound like a bad idea. Call me crazy, but if I could draw up a scenario where it'd be most beneficial to wear a seatbelt, this is it.

I think it's a little fucked up that a few bullies from grade school cost Princess Di her life.

Dudes Who Drive Convertibles

Have you ever popped the top, took the pedal to the metal, and watched your luscious locks flow blissfully in the wind? If so, there's a reason why I don't know you. Dudes who drive convertibles are ultimate tool bags.

Every time I see one coming my way, I pray their car is involved in a serious safety recall, except they never find out about it.

Non-Handicapped Assholes Who Use the Handicap Tag on Their Car

I see way too many people parking in the handicap spot who look perfectly able. Maybe they're driving someone else's car, but just because they have a disabled person's tag, should they still be allowed to park in this luxurious spot?

I think a handicap person needs more than a hang tag on their rearview mirror these days, because too many people are taking advantage of the system. I have no idea what actually qualifies someone as being legally handicapped, but when I see a Tesla parked in the first spot, something's not right. This is either the coolest handicapped person ever, or realistically, it's just some douchebag who got their hands on a tag, felt nothing putting it up, and was completely satisfied to walk ten feet into the store.

From here on out, cops should tow any car parked in a handicap spot to force the owner out of the store. If it turns out to be a legitimately disabled driver, even better, the car can be dropped off in the fire zone just three steps from the door.

Stage Dancers for Pop Stars

Watch these people. They're hilarious. Any time there's a performer on stage, a large group of "dancers" come out and awkwardly surround the main entertainer. Usually the singer is already wearing one of the most ridiculous things you've ever seen, but leave it to the dancers to come out in something even more stupid. Who are these people, and why are they here? Are their arm twirls and leg kicks enhancing the performance in any way? These people couldn't be more worthless.

If there's a need to distract the viewer's eye from time to time, then why not play videos of snakes preying in the wild? This would make as much sense as a bunch of goofy people turning flips all over the stage. Actually, a snake makes even more sense, because it's already been established as a staple during a pop star's performance. That's another thing I don't get. Why are we putting boa constrictors on non-talented, semi-attractive pop stars? Is this hot? Should this turn me on?

I assume the manager's just hoping for another Steve Irwin-like disaster to rid themselves of their client's nonsense.

People Who Fight

"I disagree with what you're saying. Therefore, I'm going to punch you."

The concept of fighting is almost as stupid as a backup dancer. Seeing a fight build from scratch is something else. It starts out as a useless conversation that goes too far between a couple jackasses who think they're tougher than each other. This conversation can range from something as simple as naming the second baseman for the Colorado Rockies, to being called out for double penetrating an ex-girlfriend's sister. That's the beauty of it. The fight will be just as intense regardless of whether it's about the first or second subject.

I don't see why this is, time and time again, a solution for so many people. If you win, what happens next? You get the girl and have mind-blowing animal sex? And by animal sex, I mean two forty-something's with ponytails back-dooring you in the holding cell.

People Who Set Their Clocks Ahead So They Aren't Late

I've done it. But I set it back after I thought about it for more than two seconds and realized how stupid it was.

I'm still trying to figure out why I actually did this. I, like everyone else, set my clock ahead so I'd be on time for work. It took about three days before I woke up and realized I could hit the snooze button another time. Do we honestly think we won't pick up on this? Do we really think we'll believe the actual time is ten minutes from now?

When I did it, I only changed my bedroom clock, since it's my alarm in the morning. Bad move. It bit me in the ass when I was saucing this girl a few months ago. She peeked at my bedroom clock beforehand, and then caught a glimpse of another clock on her way to the bathroom. It was the first time she'd ever had sex for negative five minutes. And that included three eat out minutes.

Popular Song Lyrics

After painfully listening to Owl City's "Fireflies" for the 32nd time, I'm officially convinced the lyrics of a song have absolutely no impact on its success. It's impossible to listen to any song in the top 25 and not want to kill yourself. All people care about is one thing, and one thing only: "the beat." Gone are the days when little girls would have slumber parties and belt out the latest Hanson song with their hairbrush. Instead, they're jamming out to songs like "Last Friday Night" by Katy Perry. *Last Friday night. We went streaking in the park. Skinny dipping in the dark. Then had a ménage à trois.* Katy Perry fans are eight years old. It's no wonder girls dress the way they do on Halloween.

And then there are songs where no one in their right mind could decipher the words unless they were being read from a piece of paper. But it doesn't matter. If you're riding with the tune and feeling the flow, you're good to go. Could you be dancing to songs about baby killing and bestiality? Probably. You'd never know.

Slow it down a bit. Know what you're getting into first.

Plane Rules

We all know how miserable it is to fly. The small seats, fat people, babies, and lack of hot flight attendants are enough to make flying awful, but there are other things that are just as terrible.

The shared armrest. The minute I step into a plane, go to a movie, or share a seat next to someone I've never met, I know full well I'm not getting that armrest. It may be because I'm not aggressive enough, but it's probably more so because I don't want to graze the random dude to my right. Having your bare arm brush up against a disgusting old man is like having your public bathroom TP fall off the seat just before your cheeks touch down.

From the get-go, sitters should have an open conversation about armrest likes and dislikes. Be honest about it. Maybe you're a front of the armrest type of guy. Maybe the back. If one likes the front and one likes back, *bam*, you're good to go. Four hours of smooth sailing. If you share the same passion for the back, a timeshare should be put in play. Thirty minutes each, back and forth. You go, they go. I know it's not perfect, but it's better than cupping your genitals for four hours.

———∿∿———

Exiting a plane definitely takes way too long. It shouldn't take twenty minutes for seventy-five people to walk seventy-five feet. What are you doing when the plane lands? Do you not know to gather your things before the doors open? Pack up your computer, put your iPad away, grab your bag from the overhead, and go. It's not that hard. For some reason I always get stuck behind the grandma who hasn't flown in thirty-five years. She somehow brought three carryon bags onto the plane and is more concerned about putting eight sweaters on so she doesn't get chilly while walking through the jet bridge for fifteen seconds. Plus, she's probably in town to see her grandson's terrible kindergarten play, so I hate her even more now.

———∿∿———

The people that sprint to their feet as soon as the seatbelt sign goes off are fun. If I'm stuck somewhere for 20 minutes and had my choice between sitting and standing, there wouldn't even be a discussion.

It's awesome when the person two rows behind you storms up the aisle to strengthen their position in line.

Are these people for real? Planes operate with a standard row system for a reason. This isn't anything new. At this point, I'm praying for a tarmac delay. Anything that puts these douchebags back in their seats is fine with me.

Why do some people stay on the plane and wait? What are they waiting for? You're here. You can't go any further. If you're willing to convince yourself that you'd rather be stuck on an airplane versus getting home to your wife and kids after a five day business trip, then she must be atrocious.

On the plus side, the airplane blower is a tremendous thing. Have you ever let it loose? Those things are powerful. I use mine to mask my man-queefs. Hands down, that's THE best thing about flying. You can sit there all day and unleash at will. Quietly aim your blower towards the stink, and boom, it's gone. Never seen, never known. But sometimes it goes away too quickly and I start to miss it. We all love our own brand.

Jennifer Aniston

She played a key role in one of my all-time favorite movies (Office Space), is extremely hot, and is either continuously horny, or very, very cold. She has the hardest nipples of any girl on the planet.

Why, you ask? I think it's pretty simple. Before she goes on camera she must spend a good amount of time in the makeup room, right? Makeup rooms generally have mirrors. People can generally see themselves in mirrors. I don't think it has anything to do with her outfit, temperature, or co-star. Once she sneaks a peek of herself, her nipples simultaneously sneak a peek through her top.

If you catch her in a scene and they aren't out, take a closer look at her makeup. It's probably time for a touchup.

Trying Someone Else's Food

This is one of the few situations where you are—no matter what—expected to lie 100 percent of the time. The person offering has already decided their food is good. But for some reason they have to get your approval on it as well, just to make sure. It goes something like this:

"Oh wow, this is amazing, you have to try this." Mid-sentence, the person offering will already be halfway to your plate, ready to drop their food off in a spot you had strategically cleared for your own eating game plan. Automatically, you must try it, swallow it, and like it. It could be the taste equivalent of having a foreign object lodged in your corn hole, but you must indisputably respond, "Wow, you're right, that is good."

You'll reply, "Wanna try mine?" Now here's the thing. The giver can opt out if the taster has not previously stated an enjoyment for his or her own food.

Always make the first move. Put yourself in a position to turn down her Kung Pao Chicken. You don't want your date to know this early on that you're allergic to peanuts. But if it comes down to it, just eat it. You're better off having her think all of the swelling, wheezing, cramps, vomiting, and diarrhea is from the cat ("chicken") you just inhaled. Don't even think about telling her you're allergic to a peanut. They're so tiny, round, and innocent. The only thing weaker would be an allergy to a cotton ball.

No girl wants to blow a pussy.

Bill, Not Check

You're out to dinner with the lady having a glorious evening. You're each a few bites away from clearing your plate and things are wrapping up nicely. The waitress notices you're done, comes over, and this fun little conversation is triggered:

"So, how was everything this evening?"

"Good, very good, thank you."

You have no choice but to say how great your meal was. Have you ever said what you actually wanted to? I haven't. Six times out of ten I want to say, "Eh, it was all right, not your best, but OK." No one does, though. The waitress hears the meal was flawless 98 percent of the time. In her mind, Friendly's is the finest restaurant in the world. Actually, it is. Any place that serves clam strips, French fries, and ice cream on the same plate is a gem.

The waitress continues …

"Do you guys care for dessert, maybe some coffee?"

After giggling and looking at each other for a second, you'll ultimately say, "I don't think so, we're pretty stuffed. We'll just take the check, thank you."

The waitress will completely understand the request, but it makes no sense at all. What kind of check are we asking for? As far as I know, a check is written by an individual who's trying to purchase something. You don't get paid to have free food served to you.

It's a bill, not a check.

"I don't think so, we're pretty stuffed. I think we'll just take the bill, thank you."

Ah, much better. Even if you think I'm an idiot for caring about this, you at least have to agree with me that the noun version of "check" should be deleted from the English language. There's nothing more useless in today's society. We have to get rid of it now before its only meaning becomes something it was never meant to be in the first place.

Anyway, say your food was great, you're full, you don't want dessert, and you would like the bill. Your waitress will never know the clam strips tasted just as awful the second time around.

Restaurant Specials

Can these please be written down and handed out along with the regular menu in every restaurant from here on out moving forward? I know they don't change and I'm sick and tired of awkwardly making eye contact while nodding my head and pretending there's the slightest chance I'm going to order, let alone remember anything that's mentioned.

"Ooohhhh, yummy." "Mmmmm, that sounds amazing." "Oh babe, we should definitely try that."

Nope. It never happens, and it never will. I'd rather spend those two minutes continuously dropping bowling balls onto my bare feet.

"A" As In

I was on the phone the other day and started playing the first-letter word game. You know the one—where you use the letter you're trying to spell by saying another word beginning with that letter?

I don't know who started the "S" as in "Sally" concept, but I'm ready to spice up it up a bit. What if we began saying things like "B" as in "Bag of dicks" or "T" as in "Tingle"? You can keep it as clean or unclean as you like, but wouldn't it be way better if we turned the "Sally" and "Nancy" concept into "Fisting" and "Coleslaw"? Or you could really mess with the customer service rep and drop a "P" as in "Pneumonia."

Maybe it'll give you a giggle, but more importantly, maybe it'll give the dude who sits at a desk from 9 to 5 and hears "A as in Apple" 57 times a day a break.

Even though an imbecile could make out "Dan" over the phone, I play the first-letter word game every time.

"D" as in "Dick snot", "A" as in "A", "N" as in "Nickleback."

Kiss

The band. People say great things, they've been around forever, and I've heard of Gene Simmons. I don't doubt they're extremely talented and play a mean guitar, but I can't wrap my head around their appeal. Maybe it's the leather pants that throw me off. Although I usually love guys in makeup with bulging penises, I like my penises a little younger.

But for real, why are they taken seriously? Did anyone ever question the attire? What are they wearing? Why are their faces painted? And why is everyone OK with this?

You don't see Josh Groban all dolled up. Just sing the song.

Animal Siblings

It's a simple rule. Don't sleep with someone you're related to. If you do, you'll have a messed up baby. But does this rule apply to animals? It must, right?

We, as humans, know who we're related to. We also have pretty decent memories and will still know who our brother is after a weeklong vacation. But I'm pretty sure animals don't have this same capacity. They know each other for a little while after birth, but once they split up to grab a bite, there's no way they remember who their cousin is when they get back.

It may be wrong to say, but every animal looks identical. Which means there's a good chance they're hooking up with blood relatives on a pretty frequent basis. But does the same sibling-on-sibling rule apply to them?

What we once thought of as rabies might be something completely different. Is the animal slow? Yep. Is it unfazed by humans? Yep. Is it uncontrollably drooling? Yep. Does it look like it belongs in a white trailer park? Yep.

Rabies no more. You, sir, simply have an inbred rabbit.

Clean, Dirty Words

There are quite a few words that have become derogatory over the last ten years or so. Here are a few:

- Mary

- Nancy

- Floppy Disk

- Taco

- Flames

- Salami

- Rubber

- Coming

- Prairie Dog

- Wheelbarrow

- Fist

- Fruitcake

- Backpack

My brother and I used to play "wheelbarrow" and push

each other around for hours when we were younger. We'd go all night until my mom rang the dinner bell and called us in. In hindsight, I guess we shouldn't have yelled back, "coming".

Jockeys

Not the undies…the short, middle-age men who come from god-knows-where and ride the hell out of horses. Why are they so small, and why are they so good at riding horses?

This was always a "job" I was especially fond of. If I can sit on top of an animal, beat the living shit out of it, and make money doing it, sign me up.

What possibly makes someone any better at this than someone else? Jockeys are like race car drivers: un-athletic athletes who can only turn left. You just know these are the type of guys who leave a few drops in the milk carton before putting it back in the fridge. Why would they care? They know someone else will come along and do the dirty work for them. In this case, it's their wife. But during the day, it's their horse or engine.

Adults Riding in Cars

Adults ride in cars together pretty frequently. But from time to time, you'll see three or more adults walking to a car. What do they do? How is the front seat decided upon? Ultimately, one of these 40-somethings has to pull the seat bar forward, bend down, and climb into the back seat.

I love seeing a pack of four hauling down the freeway in a '98 Corolla. This is the optimal car for an adult-riding-in-the-back-seat spotting. The windows are nowhere close to being tinted, and second row legroom is nowhere to be found. Here they are, two well-respected individuals, possibly with a family, maybe even a pet, staring aimlessly out the second row window. Meanwhile, the two adults who snagged the front are talking carefree, as if there's no one else in the car.

Let's face it. No one looks back when they're in a car. The folks in the front own the conversation. So adult or not, if you're in the rear, just do yourself a favor and shut up.

Closed Captioning

What's off limits when it comes to sponsorship? Does closed captioning really need to be provided by someone? The fact that TV stations make money off a feature that supports deaf people and Hispanics is a complete joke.

I can't believe they haven't whored out famous landmarks yet. The Statue of Liberty brought to you by Exxon. Give it a few more years.

Albert Pujols

Hands down the greatest last name out there.

Car Dealership Flags

Where do they get these things and why are they so big? The American flag in front of the White House would get laughed at in comparison. At this point, it's pretty clear that all car dealerships and all car companies are fanatics about America.

But seventy-five percent of these companies aren't even close to American. Why does Kia throw up the red, white, and blue in front of their store? We get it—you're proud to be an Asian American selling Asian cars in America.

Ironically, Asian dealerships have the biggest flags, and Toyota is king of the castle. We appreciate the foreign patriotism, but planting an oversized American flag on the front lawn is like getting busy with a girl in Spanx. At first it was appreciated, but once you peak under the hood, you quickly realize scheduled maintenance hasn't been followed for years.

Bedding

Two of the best investments you can make in life are buying a huge-ass TV and an obnoxiously large and comfortable bed. That's 16 hours/day right there. Times 365 days a year. Times 60 years of post-purchase enjoyment. Swap them out every ten years and you'll have spent about 20 grand for 350,400 hours of magic. That, my friends, is a smart investment.

I love my bed, but you won't find me buying 15 oddly shaped decorative pillows to match my down comforter. You wake up, make your bed, go to work, unmake your bed, masturbate in your bed, go to sleep, and repeat. Why do people spend money on decorative pillows? Master bedrooms are almost always off limits. No adult invites another adult to "check out" his or her place of rest. It's not a great room or kitchen.

No one will ever see or care about your bed, but keep tossing those pillows off night after night so you can arrange them again in the morning.

That reminds me...

Poor Investments

- Excessive pillows for your bed
- Varsity jackets
- Class rings
- Clothes between the ages of 2-16
- Gifts for girlfriends
- Halloween costumes
- The "no touch" room
- Bras while boobs are still growing
- Action figures
- Toys for children
- Any accessory ever made
- Private schools
- Paying for music
- Gym memberships
- Sports lessons
- Piano lessons

- Anything white people spend money on

- Not owning bowling shoes

Hibernation

Every October, the breeze gets stiffer and leaves start dancing to the ground everywhere around you. There's no doubt this is one of the most refreshing times of year. The autumn air reeks of apple cider and football. Slow and dark days may lie ahead, but for now, life is good.

In the midst of pumpkin-carving and apple-pie-making, animals all over, from ladybugs to grizzly bears, work overtime in preparation for their winter slumber. They carefully store every nut and berry they uncover before the start of the inevitable and unbearable winter season.

Hibernation blows my mind. Google I'm Feeling Lucky just told me the American black bear can sleep uninhibited for a hundred days without waking up. Get the fuck out of here. How is this real? How do these things not die? I call bullshit to the whole three days without water and three weeks without food nonsense. How is this not one of the most researched activities out there? This blows every health science theory out of the water, but it gets breezed over in every classroom and Planet Earth episode.

Can we hibernate? If they can, why can't we? If you think you've ever had a solid night's sleep, can you even begin to imagine how exquisite it would be to wake up after a 116-day nap?

If you ever wanted to cum on someone's face, a post-hibernation facial would make it way more impactful.

Handicap Stall

The handicap bathroom stall is undeniably the most popular stall in the bathroom to take a poop in. If that bathroom suite's open, I'm going in.

Why doesn't the handicap stall warrant the same level of respect as the handicap parking spot? Unless you're a scumbag with a fake tag, no one actually parks in a coveted blue spot. But this same level of consideration is thrown out the window when any ordinarily abled human being enters a restroom. You won't get much of an argument from me, though, because how many times have you actually seen someone on wheels go potty? I'm still at zero. And until I see one, it'll continue to be my stall of choice every time.

But what happens if you actually run into one? Think about it…

You just slammed a cheese steak, fries, and a milkshake. You have another one of those "I ate a boatload of food and it has absolutely nowhere to go because my body hasn't gotten rid of the previous meal yet" types of poop cravings. At this point, you're locked in. You walk into the bathroom feeling good. Luckily, every stall is vacant, so you zone in on the roomy, spacious, and suspiciously cleaner handicap stall. You zip in, zip down, throw some TP on the seat, and get to work. Immediately following the initial poop splash into the bowl, you hear the bathroom door open. But this time, there are no footsteps. Only wheels.

After a series of awkward knocks, you must respond. The chair clearly can't fit into any other stall, so the person is left sitting there, comfortably, in prime position to wait you out. What do you do? What's your excuse?

Since I'm chairless, I play deaf. I take my time, wipe 'til it's only white, and mumble a few words on the way out to reinforce the deafness. I think that warrants the use of a handicap stall, right?

Holding Doors

Anytime someone's ten steps behind you, you have to open the door, hold it for a few seconds, and wait for the person to receive your gracious gesture.

I used to be a holder, but not anymore. If I know there will be no interruption between my natural open and close, then I have nothing against the door hold. But if you think I'm going to stand there and wait for your sorry ass to catch up, there's a strong chance you also think swimming in lakes is fun.

My door holding days are officially behind me. I got sick of holding a door for a person who's never as appreciative as they should be. I have places to be. Let's say you hold two doors a day, at three seconds per hold, that's over thirty minutes a year. What would you do with your extra thirty minutes?

Oh, that's a lot less weird than what I would do.

A few more thoughts:

What's the breaking point, distance wise, between waiting for the door hold and ignoring the person behind you?

Isn't it the worst when you're on the receiving end of the hold, but there are two doors? The first thank you after the initial hold couldn't be more routine than urinating, but what do you do after the second consecutive hold? Is an additional thank you necessary? I think it is, but I always feel like a jackass saying it. You have to be careful. Make sure the second thank you is audible, but make sure it's at a volume that's much, much lower than the initial thank you. That way, it'll alleviate the awkwardness, but the holder will still know their additional gesture wasn't assumed.

Commence

Am I the only one who's disgusted by the definition of this word? There's not a more perfect word to mean "the end of something."

This is obviously how it should be defined:

Com·mence

1. To stop something, or anything

2. To halt an event

3. To commence

Now here's the real definition straight from the good folks at Merriam Webster:

Com·mence

1. To enter upon: begin

2. To have or make a beginning: start

Now get this.

Com·mence·ment

1. The ceremony of conferring degrees or granting diplomas at the end of the academic year

Interesting. Commence means to begin something. Commencement means a ceremony to end something. Apparently the noun's an antonym of the verb. What am I missing? And don't give me the "graduation means the beginning of the next chapter" theory. That's bull crap. The dictionary isn't supposed to read that much into a word.

I wouldn't know where to start to change the definition of a word, but it's certainly something worth putting a little effort into.

Who invented all of our words anyway? Whoever signed the final papers to put "cunty" in the dictionary is a genius.

Mount Rushmore

I'm still not convinced this actually exists. So you're telling me that four of the greatest presidents in the history of this country are sculpted into the side of a mountain that covers 1,278 acres, and is virtually perfect? Sure thing...

I have to admit, it would be awesome if it was real. But come on, it's "located" in South Dakota. This should be an immediate red flag. Why would they put the world's greatest mountain carving in a state that 99.6 percent of Americans couldn't locate on a map? What makes the story even more ludicrous is apparently some Danish guy and his son built it. Right.

Mount Rushmore is a load of crap. Just like Bert from Sesame Street. What an uptight prick. I'm glad everyone thought Bert and Ernie were banging, though, because it got Bert banned from TV. But let's be honest—there's no way Ernie would have gotten down with that. Bert may have been tight, but his baggage definitely outweighed the pleasure.

Meeting People

I hate meeting people. You can never be yourself.

Three-quarters of the people I know and am close to have been in my life since elementary school. The other quarter were based on drunken relationships that evolved throughout college. But to be fair, college isn't real life, so I never had to go through the misery of formally meeting those individuals.

Isn't it great when you're at a party and your girlfriend wants you to meet someone she went to high school with? The person you're being introduced to couldn't be more meaningless, but you're still forced to meet Melanie, her tennis partner from seven years ago. And she isn't even hot.

Once in a while you'll meet someone who may actually have an impact on your life. Meeting your college roommate freshman year is a prime example. I strategically bypassed this by living with someone I'd known since kindergarten, so I never had to worry about it. But, there are still many out there who do.

Everyone, when meeting anyone, is fake. Trying to forge a relationship with someone based on a toned-down version of yourself is miserable. You can never relax. You're constantly on edge, trying to make sure you maintain the bunk relationship you've created. But in the long run, all you want to do is casually say, "Fuck that guy," whenever you see Sheldon from the Big Bang Theory on TV. But you simply can't say it. You have no idea how the other person may react.

Why can't everyone be straight up from the beginning? Conversations like this should happen much earlier.

Me: "Man, this movie stinks like old vagina. I thought watching a bunch of couples at a retreat would be way more interesting. Let's play poop dollar instead."

New Friend: "Already on it. The pizza is on order so the delivery dude should be here in 20. I'm prairie dogging so grab me a five and I'll make Abe's face brown in no time."

Me: "You complete me."

If this could happen, I would love meeting people. Right off the bat you'll know whether or not you actually give a shit about the person standing next to you.

Toothpaste

After years of toothpaste experience, I know exactly what tube I need for that everyday clean feeling. But for some reason, I feel the need to explore new flavors whenever I need a refill. The whitening, tarter control, mouthwash-infused toothpastes continue to impress me. Throw in a few different paste colors, and this category refuses to let you down.

Crest or Colgate. Whitening or Tartar Control. Peppermint or Spearmint. This should be it. Across all brands, there should be six options. But no, I walk in and buy a tube of Aquafresh striped cherry mint whitening peroxide with Scope. I'm silly.

My last toothpaste complaint is simple. The caps. Why aren't all caps connected to the tube? Why even bother with the screw-on cap? This thing tumbles onto the counter, spins around and either ends up on the floor, in the toilet, in the garbage can, or down the sink. From start to finish, I challenge you to finish a tube with the screw-on cap. There's no doubt your tube ends up unprotected no later than a quarter of the way through.

If you were to ask me if I'd rather use protection on my toothpaste tube or my ding-dong, nine times out of ten I'd say my toothpaste tube. A baby can always be aborted, but the dried up sticky paste that results from poor toothpaste tube management can be very irritating.

The National Debt

This may be the worst financial benchmark that was ever created. Correct that; it's not even close. The U.S. is 20 trillion dollars in debt. To who? Ourselves? Why does this matter and do we actually think we can do something to get rid of it? I can't begin to imagine how much money this actually is, but it seems like a lot, and it seems like it's going to be a problem for a pretty substantial amount of time. We should relax, though, because it obviously doesn't have a real impact on anything that matters.

I'm pretty sure Clinton had his hand in most of this. 20 trillion dollars can buy a shitload of blowjobs and weed. I'm sure he didn't inhale though. Better yet, she probably didn't either. She looks like the definition of a spitter.

New Things

Buying shit is awesome. The second you buy something, everything becomes more exciting. The actual content is only half the reason why I buy something to begin with. I buy shit so I can open it up. The opening up process of a shrink-wrapped electronic is one of the most enjoyable experiences out there. Finding the perfect edge of plastic gives me a boner every time out. I go more out of my way to preserve the condition of a box than I do my body when I'm soaping up in the shower. I'm very lackluster when it comes to full body coverage. Do people actually reach down and wash their toes every time they're in there?

The smell of a freshly opened product is like no other on the planet. It's better than new car and gasoline combined. It reeks of goodness. I can't explain it. The only smell that rivals it is the book or instruction manual that comes with it. Open it up, find the middle, and get in there. I smell all of my new purchases for a solid five minutes before I even think about the thing I spent money on. For a short while, all is forgotten and life is good.

The smell of a freshly opened instruction book is hands down the most miraculous smell on Earth. I can almost taste the fingers of the 11-year-old Asian who packed it.

Stuff That's Given Away

I'm fed up with the "giving-away rules" that have formed over the last 100 years. Case in point:

Ground ball down the line. The over-privileged dude sitting in the foul line chair boots it, picks it up, and starts scanning the stands to see who he'll give it to. His preference in order:

1. Girl between the age of 2-11

2. Boy between the age of 3-12

3. Hot girl between the age of 16-18, 23-27 (let's face it, college girls look beat up, so they're out)

4. Old person (most likely 70+)

5. Keep the ball

6. Any dude between the age of 17-69

The fans that actually give a shit, buy the tickets, wear the team's apparel, and drink the most beer are constantly getting screwed. What's so great about children and women? The last time I checked, the Panama Canal was still man-made.

Rest Stops

I love rest stops, especially the ones that feature nothing more than a vending machine and a guy and girls bathroom. There's never any lollygagging or horseplay. Relieve yourself and go. People have never been more efficient.

Everyone should be in a pissy travel mood, but they're not. People are happier here. And I'm one of them. I've started forcing poops so I can enjoy these treasures. Sure, I may get sexually assaulted or robbed, but it's worth it every time.

My only qualm with the rest stop, and most public bathrooms, is the size of the toilet paper. Thin TP can be remedied with multiple layers, but an underwhelming width causes many unneeded problems. They're basically asking you to slip mid-wipe. Which is ironic, because the damn soap dispensers are almost always empty.

One slip, no soap, not good. At least you won't need to stop for a chocolate bar on the way out anymore.

Double Cheek Greeting

If you've ever executed the double-sided cheek-touch greeting, there's a good chance I hate you. It's not the 19th century and you're not in France. Get over yourself.

I butt touch. Stand back to back. Lean in with the left cheek. Then lean in with the right. Embrace the contact and enjoy. If it's executed in perfect unison, it's breathtaking. Pretty soon, air kissing aristocrats will feel like a bunch of idiots once the butt-touch starts gaining steam.

Try it at your next family party. You'll finally be able to creep on your hot cousin without a second look.

Fancy Silverware

Who needs five forks to eat a meal? What am I supposed to do with the one that's above my plate? Why is every utensil a different size? Who uses spoons? Does this unusual setup account for lefties? Does the drink have to stay on the right? What happens if I want to reuse the fork I had because I was in a groove?

They take care of every unnecessary detail when it comes to silverware, but they forget one simple and fundamental thing. There's only one napkin. I have nothing against the napkin-on-lap theory, but is it that hard to throw another napkin into the mix so you don't have to continuously wipe your dirty mouth into your lap? A side napkin would solve everything.

The only question is whether it goes on the right or left side.

Speeding

I'm usually a 5-7 MPH over the speed limit kind of guy. It's enough over to feel like you're going faster than you should, but not fast enough for the cops to actually care. It's like always "forgetting" to scan the most expensive item during self-checkout. It's pretty much assumed.

On a highway, serious speeders are typically doing 20 over. These chodes are always in a pickup truck or a piece of shit Honda from the 90s. You'll see four of these fuckers coast right by you if you're on a highway for more than 15 minutes. But what pisses me off is I never see these ass-clowns pulled over. I guess I'm still waiting for the "speed monitoring aircraft" to come through.

When you're on a highway, know your lane. At 7 over, I know damn well I don't belong in the far left lane. From left to right, the speed limit per lane is 80+, 75+, and 70+. You have the right to run any car off the road that's going less than 5 over. Also, add at least 20 MPH to the "speed limit" of any work zone because we all know going 45 on a highway is a joke.

The only time lane rights can be disregarded is if you're

cruising in the 3-person carpool lane. If you're willing to make yourself look that stupid in order to prolong Earth's life for one day five billion years from now, you deserve to shave five minutes off your drive time.

Office Lights

Energy has become a major issue over the last 5-10 years. Companies and consumers are more conscious than ever, and alternative energy initiatives have never been more important. Yet, we, as a society, are still missing out on some of the most fundamental ways to save energy.

Why is every light in every office building on from the hours of 8 p.m. to 6 a.m.? Isn't this when office workers are at home spending time with people they actually care about? If you drive past an office at 10p.m., it looks like their filming a battle scene from Star Wars.

I can still hear my mom now: "When you leave a room, turn off the lights you god damn worthless piece of monkey shit. The electricity bill isn't going to pay itself. Go fuck yourself." I haven't left a light on in years.

Pluto

Pluto must feel like such a jackass.

Was it really necessary for scientists to go back and redefine the word "planet"? I guess it makes sense to pay someone good money to research whether or not the word planet had been correctly defined for the last ten thousand years.

Who cares? Why does it matter whether or not Pluto is a planet? Why are people getting paid to do this? Have people been trying to prove for years that because Saturn has rings, it should also be stripped of planet status?

Now there are only 10 million 500-page textbooks that need to be reprinted. Like most volume scams, I'm sure only two or three pages will actually change. But why would the publisher care? That's a hundred bucks a pop coming their way.

Intro to History: Volume 23. It only took 23 versions to figure out the pyramids weren't actually built by slaves.

Lefties

About 10 percent of all people are left-handed. Meaning, 10 percent of all people are automatically cooler than me. I don't know what it is, but being lefty was always one of my lifelong goals. There's not a day I don't wake up and wish I was left-handed. There's just something about it. People look way cooler if they can do something well with their left hand.

If you're one of these lucky few, congratulations, and I mean that. Leverage it. It can take you places. But please, please, do not take it for granted. Just know there are so many people out there who would do anything to be in your shoes. Anything.

Who would you rather see throw a Ding Dong at a fat kid? A regular, old, fundamentally sound righty? Or a bad ass, edgy, unorthodox lefty?

Exactly.

Work Clothes

There's no denying work clothes for women are way more casual and way more comfortable than men's.

I caught onto this immediately when I was younger. On Christmas, my mom would always make me throw on a shirt and tie. After tucking in and buttoning the highest button, I would walk downstairs and see my sister wearing black sweat pants and a purple sweater. I thought she was joking. Apparently women have to change out of their pajamas and into something even more comfortable before they leave the house in the morning.

Who determined the dressing-up rules between men and women? Business casual for a man is completely different than business casual for a woman. Especially in the summer. Wool pants, shoes, and a button down vs. a sundress and flip-flops. That's poppycock. Would it hurt to look a little more presentable? Besides, they should still be thankful they're given the opportunity to work.

Relax, it's a joke.

Dance Dance Revolution

This is probably a throwback for you. Not for me. I make an effort to watch at least one DDR YouTube video every day. Few things bring more joy to my life than watching large people dominate this game. Do yourself a favor and YouTube "fat kid ddr" the next time you're browsing around.

Sure, the obese have a lot of time on their hands because they certainly aren't participating in the local rec league, but why Dance Dance Revolution? How do they move their feet so quickly?

Fat people are trendy, so I'm always trying to figure out what's next for them. I always thought every place kicker in football should be a fat, married man. They've been throwing a hotdog down a hallway their entire life.

Unneeded Jobs

Why is someone handing me a paper towel in the bathroom? Why am I supposed to pay this person? These people make a routine activity very uncomfortable. After urination, I shoot directly for the door to avoid any chance of an awkward exchange. As soon as I'm in the clear, I wipe the leftover pee onto the next friend or family member I see.

Why does someone steal my luggage, drag it ten feet through an automatic door, and expect a tip? I can extend the arm of a suitcase. Believe it or not, I can also use the wheels and roll it through a self-opening door.

Why do librarians still exist? The average age of that profession has to be pushing a hundred by now. Talk about stealing money.

All of these people need to start reinventing their jobs. For example, if I'm deucing and the paper towel guy sneaks me a few wet ones to accelerate the cleanup, he'll be five dollars richer in no time.

Dropped Calls

Official dropped call rule:

IF **YOU** MADE THE INITIAL PHONE CALL AND THE CALL IS LOST, **YOU** ARE THE ONE RESPONSIBLE FOR CALLING THE PERSON BACK. IF YOU DID NOT MAKE THE CALL, PLEASE WAIT PATIENTLY.

You're welcome.

Virginity Rules

Not "virginity is awesome." I'm talking about the rules of virginity.

The definition of virginity is a girl who's never had a penis inserted into her vagina. And vice versa for a dude. Seems simple enough. But is it?

The idea of virginity seems to be a thing of the past, but there are still a select few who give it a go. Guys and girls who pledge abstinence before marriage are doing so because they're extremely religious, or because they're scared to death how beat up their vagina or penis would get if they gave into their temptations.

Do blowjobs count against virginity? Does anal?

Let me know if this scenario seems OK to you...

A guy or girl named Sandy orally pleasures five different friends a week, puts or takes a P in the A on three of those occasions, and can still go home to Mom at the end of the week and honestly say he or she's still a virgin?

That's a loophole if I've ever seen one. And a very loose one at that.

Chinese Envy

You'd have to scour the planet to find someone who likes and enjoys the Chinese as much as I do. They epitomize the word happy. If you're lucky enough to be in the presence of a Chinese person right now, turn their way immediately and stare. They have a relentless passion for life. They simply glow.

I envy the Chinese, big time.

Although unbelievably content, I think every once and a while their lackadaisical attitude may impact their well-being. The carelessness goes a little too far every time I order the $4.95 lunch special from my local Chinese joint. It consists of an entrée, choice of brown or white rice, an egg roll, fortune cookie, some sort of Asian cracker, and way too many sauces. The fact that they charge $4.95 for all of this really concerns me. Is the meat FDA approved? Probably not. But when Ping peddles up with my food in his basket and a huge smile on his face, all my concerns immediately wash away and I'm almost as happy as he is.

Building Things

Have you ever taken a drive? Sure you have. Have you ever taken a drive down a major highway near a big city and taken in the sights? More likely than not. But have you ever stopped for one second and questioned how the hell all of this shit was built?

How was every building constructed over the past two hundred years, never mind airplanes, rocket ships, submarines, oil tankers, cruise ships, blimps, bowling alleys, ice rinks, movie theaters, Costco's, schools, stadiums, and 18-wheelers.

Didn't we put a bunch of Asians in internment camps way back when in the mid-1900s? Is it possible we enslaved every one of them to build this shit for us? There's no chance in hell a group of regular Americans could have assembled the Apollo 11 space shuttle.

There's not a doubt in my mind Armstrong beat the living piss out of Aldrin to get off that ship first.

Bidets

How much would you pay if every time you sat down to poop, you could, without thinking, just get up and walk away? What if you never had to wipe again? You would have the power of poop disappearance. You would be unstoppable. Think about all of the wasted time, headaches, and pain from the excruciating process of cleaning your bum. I offer you a lifetime of no wiping.

It's a great hypothetical. I've gotten responses anywhere from, "I would pay to keep doing it because it feels so good," to "$50,000." Where do you fall?

If you could significantly reduce your average wipe count per poop, it would be life changing. Enter the bidet. A perfectly pressurized stream of water that shoots directly up the anus. How beautiful is that? Welcome to pleasure town.

Why is this genius butt cleaning machine not more broadly adopted in the US? We're disgusting and we waste so much time on the toilet battling comeback-poops that leave brown on the TP after 22 wipes. I don't know about you, but sign me up for a bidet today.

A bidet could also be very clutch if you're yanking your

yo-yo and you need some help keeping it up. Don't pretend you haven't tried butt stuff once or twice while pleasuring yourself.

People Who Look Back

You're sitting in class. You're a good twenty minutes in. All of a sudden, the dude three rows in front of you pulls a 180, shifts his body and neck all the way around, and looks right at you.

Fuck these people. People who turn around for no reason are the worst. I'm sure you've encountered these imbeciles before. Whether it's in a class, on a bus, or at a sporting event, these people are everywhere. Why are they turning around? What are they looking for? Do they not realize the entertainment is in front of them? Are they trying to locate the emergency exit? Do they think they'll be the first to see something unexpected? Do they not realize it is super weird?

I urge you to start punching these people in the face. This needs to stop.

Elevators

The elevator is one of the most mysterious things out there. It's a lock to cause discomfort. As soon as that button's pressed, people go into shutdown mode and prepare themselves for the next minute of silence.

Please be responsible and considerate when entering an elevator. Be sure to leave plenty of room between yourself and the opening door. Believe it or not, there may be people already on the elevator that want to get off at the very stop you're getting on. I know it's crazy, but elevators are public. Step back, leave space, and once the path's clear, hop on. Take a quick peek into the reflection, pull out your phone, keep your head down, and it'll be over before you know it.

One time, a woman queefed on me in an elevator. It was fantastic. Not only did it up the awkwardness level even further, but the elevator began to smell like a dumpster full of kitten carcasses had just been vomited on.

Over 21 to Drink

Why do bars always say, "Must be over 21 to drink"? As far as I remember, I woke up in a hospital wearing a diaper holding a public urination ticket the morning after I turned 21. I have little doubt I was legally served way too much alcohol at a bar that night.

Did I also have intercourse with an oversized Somalian at some point during the evening? I'd rather not get into it. The point is I'm pretty sure you can drink if you're 21.

Close Families

I know it may be a family tradition or something, but I get weirded out when I see a dad and daughter swapping mouth kisses. Apparently some families think this is completely normal. Whether you're six or twenty-six, you're supposed to go lip on lip during every hello and goodbye greeting. Ew.

Say you're meeting your girlfriend's parents for the first time and your greeting background is handshakes, hugs, or worst case, a cheek kiss. Yet, you walk into the kitchen and watch your girl sprint over to Daddy. Daddy embraces her in his arms, picks her up, performs a spinning helicopter hug, and plants a two-second mouth kiss on her to top it off. Two minutes later, she comes over to you, thanks you for driving, and throws her tongue in your mouth in appreciation. Not cool. I've only been in her dad's presence for five minutes, and I can taste what he had for breakfast. Turns out, it was her mom.

If your family participates in these odd, incest-like greetings, there have to be some post-kiss ground rules. A mint, lozenge, stick of gum, or teeth clean isn't too much to ask. The least you can do is eat a finger full of peanut butter to mask the stank.

What would life be like if I was brought up this way? What if I had to mouth kiss my mom every time I saw her? That thought makes me very uncomfortable, because I wouldn't know what to do if it moved.

Peeing in Urinals

Do girls immediately spit and squeeze out a fart as soon as they walk into a bathroom, too?

Most gents like the urinal, but I'm in the minority. I was always taught to pee directly onto the back wall, but the pressure of my stream must be through the roof, because I've been experiencing more splash back than ever. I'm in a slump, and I'm desperately trying to get out of it.

In an effort to regain my form, I started peeing directly into the urinal cake. Little did I know, this evoked a pleasant, cherry-like aroma. Although it smelled lovely, deep into the pee, a puddle formed, and splash back was imminent.

I've been toying around with different angles and heights. I've also attempted sitting on the lip, but it doesn't feel right. I'm lost. There has to be a more forgiving backboard out there, but I haven't found it yet.

These days, I have good bathroom trips and bad bathroom trips. Walking out with damp pants is one thing, but it's even worse if you accidentally see a dick in the next urinal over.

Passing on the Message

Why do people waste their time saying things like, "Send him my best," or "Tell her I said hi"?

The people putting in these requests couldn't be more meaningless. As soon as they walk away, they're immediately forgotten. There's a reason why the absentee hasn't put forth any effort to see or talk to these losers.

Enough nonsense. If you're asked this question again, just be honest and explain that you will either:

A) Never remember you had the conversation.

Or

B) Let them know the person on the receiving end wouldn't give two shits about the message in the first place.

Honorary Degrees

It's graduation day. You're sitting in the crowd, clean-shaven with a new haircut, the folks are here, and you're feeling good. You just finished an epic 4-7 years of college and are ready for real life. You've spent endless nights studying, reading, writing, and meeting with classmates. You survived a few 8 a.m. classes and ended up on the better side of a 3.0. You worked your ass off for one thing: a degree. This degree should be the key to your future, the key to a job, and the key to success.

Turns out, you busted your ass for nothing. The guest speaker comes on, and you soon realize all you needed to do to earn a degree is give a shitty five minute "You can accomplish anything you put your mind to" speech. The guest speaker is then greeted by the dean and verbally ejaculated on before being presented with a complimentary business degree. Just like that, you and the CFO from JCPenney are educationally equal. Fuck that.

I don't think that's the best example to set for the youngsters in the crowd. Since degrees are obviously worthless, now your impressionable little brother will drop out of school and move to Nashville to chase his musical dreams like an idiot.

Nevertheless, I'd be even more pissed about honorary degrees had Tim "The Tool Man" Taylor not received one from Western Michigan University. That was just awesome, and well deserved.

Nose Maintenance

Whether you admit it or not, everyone picks. If you're one of those who claim to get everything out with a tissue, you're a liar. It's impossible to flush out every piece of nose garbage while blowing. With so many nooks and crannies, there's always a boog wedged in no man's land.

There's no way around it. You have to pick. The tissue blow is just a wasted step to begin with. Everything instantly becomes wet, making it much grosser when you inevitably have to go in and clean up with the finger.

I'm still trying to figure out why people have so much hate for the pick. It's not a secret. By now, it's commonly known that picking runs rampant among man, woman, and child.

I think everyone should pick freely. If you can, wash your hands when you're done. If not, oh well. You probably don't wash your hands after you pee anyway, so why fuss about a little nose ejaculation?

Have some fun with it. Wipe it on a friend.

Children's Author

Being a children's author has to be, without a doubt, the easiest job on the planet.

Let's think about it:

- The book is no more than 15 pages long

- The book has no more than three lines per page

- The book is 75% pictures

- The book is filled with words containing no more than six letters

- The book must have a plot that can be followed by a three-year old

Seems difficult. I'm going to give myself five minutes to write one. Here we go:

Sammy the Snail Slithers South

Seven Munson

This is Sammy the Snail.

A storm is brewing.

"Oh no," says Sammy.

Drip, drop, drip, drop … psssshhh
goes the wind.

What to do? Where to go?

Looks like it's time to slither south.

Rumble rumble rumble ...

Out of the brush, a peculiar rhino appears.

"Hey little buddy, need a lift?" questions the rhino.

"That would be swell," says Sammy. "You're the kindest rhino I've ever met."

"Call me Ralph," says Ralph.

"OK, Ralph," says Sammy.

"Shall we?" says Ralph.

"Yes," says Sammy.

Now the best of friends, Ralph and Sammy
begin their journey.

And just like that, Sammy gets south much faster.

There's a good chance that was the easiest thing I've ever done in my life. But at the end of the day, it has no shot. It's 16 pages.

Pirates

Remember when pirates used to be cool? Sure, they did their fair share of theft, but everyone seems to overlook that. Pirate costumes continue to be a staple for kids on Halloween. Everyone "awwws" whenever they see a six-year-old with an eye patch and a dagger. The old school pirate continues to impress youngsters and elders alike.

The perception of the modern day pirate isn't as favorable. What a piece of shit everyone thinks these people are. Instead of cool outfits and talking birds, they have ripped up sweat pants and handguns. I'm pretty sure it's the gun that's made the modern day pirate a bit more unpopular. Anyone who can pull a trigger is a cop-out. Sword duels are much cooler and much more likable.

Nevertheless, I still don't get the whole idea of pirating. It's 2018. How do pirates still exist? How do they actually steal 500-foot long tankers? Aren't there enough people on board to avoid this sort of attack?

Don't forfeit and hand over your keys the second a raft pulls up next to you with six leisurely dressed males. I'm sure they're just mid-bake and need to borrow a cup of milk or a scoop of sugar.

The Mirror Look

I don't know about you, but I absolutely love looking at myself in the mirror. After years and years of fine tuning, my mirror look is now complete. It was an awfully long and sometimes painful journey, but it was definitely worth it. From here on out, I can perfectly arrange my jaw, cheeks, lips, and eyebrows in flawless unison. I look amazing.

It's much easier waking up in the morning knowing you can temporarily trick yourself into believing you're actually attractive. It certainly boosts my self-esteem, that's for sure. I only hope your mirror look is going as smoothly as mine.

There is a limit though. The mirror look can add no more than 3 points to your 10 point hot score. So if you're starting below a 4, you're better off removing all mirrors from your home.

That's what Steven Tyler must have done.

A Flurry of Questions

1. Why are the stickers on new things always so hard to get off?

2. What happened to the days when SNL used to be funny?

3. When did fortune cookies stop being fortune cookies?

4. Why do farts smell and burps don't?

5. Why has the NBA never put together a one-on-one tournament?

6. Why is Lou Holtz still allowed on TV?

7. What does the "+3" years mean when someone is sentenced to life in prison +3 years?

8. Why can't professional athletes squirt the Gatorade into their own mouths?

9. Why don't hotel remotes ever come with a guide?

10. Where do superheroes change?

11. When called, how often is the fire truck actually used?

12. Why do people wear suits out on a Saturday night?

13. Why do people wear snow hats inside?

14. Why don't trains move as fast as they can?

15. What are the IQs of people who watch soap operas?

16. What are the IQs of people who keep psychics open?

17. Who uses anything but a #2 pencil?

18. Who uses pencils?

19. Do people realize the commitment of getting a tattoo?

20. Why are Comedy Central comedians never funny?

21. Why do figure skating outfits look the way they do?

22. Why do people think you can't wash your car if it's going to rain?

23. How can that guy say "Wrapped up like a douche" in that song?

24. Why do people call the northernmost central part of the US the Midwest?

25. Why do some people smell?

26. How do people get into doing porn?

27. What's the first day like?

28. What's the career path to become a professional tickler?

29. Why is there always lint in my belly button?

30. Why are there always lanes blocked for construction with no construction?

31. Why is someone who's left out 'chopped liver'?

32. Why do abandoned cars always have a bag in the window?

33. Where do they get the bag?

34. Why are actresses now called actors?

35. Why are lesbians now called gays?

36. Who invented "Dayoh" at baseball games?

37. Why do old people always dress up?

38. Why do people crack their car window when it's raining?

39. Why do I always want to eat lava whenever I see it?

40. Why can't the pitcher catch the pop-up?

41. What's the difference between mostly sunny and partly cloudy?

42. Why don't all boxers have a button?

43. What if the pilot has to poop?

44. Why do birds always have diarrhea?

45. Why aren't weather forecasts ever accurate?

46. How is a 50 percent chance of rain beneficial to my planning?

47. What's the point of the crew team member who doesn't paddle?

48. Why is Drew Carey such a bad host on *The Price is Right*?

49. What's the point of cutting your nails over a garbage can?

50. Why does a sign that says "Park in the Rear" make me giggle?

51. Why is there still poop on the TP after so many wipes?

52. How can the Chips Ahoy serving size of one cookie be taken seriously?

53. At what age does it start to get weird if you see your dad naked?

54. What are people lifting weights for?

55. Why do gas stations sell roses?

56. Why do so many people not have EZ Pass?

57. Why do people think taking a bath gets you clean?

58. How are there only two sides in politics?

59. Why do people put stuffed animals above the back seat of their car?

60. Is it really necessary to wear a mask at an airport?

61. Why are banana peels so slippery in cartoons?

62. Why are the unpopped popcorn nutritional facts included on the microwave popcorn label?

Chickenpox

Have you had it yet? I hope so, because if you're reading this, you're likely over the age of 11. And if you haven't had chickenpox by 11, you're 150 times more likely to die while battling this disease.

Actually, that probably isn't true at all.

Chickenpox never made sense to me though. How can you only get something once, and why do you have to be between the ages of three and eight to get it? This leaves me with many more questions:

- What piece of shit chicken started this?

- Why does any illness ending in "pox" sound so deadly?

- Are there people out there who will never get it?

- Are there people out there who will get it multiple times?

- How does the "pox" know to target children?

- Is this is the only sickness parents love seeing their kids get?

- Do you get the bubble gum medicine?

- What's the plural of chickenpox?
- What if you die before you get it?

Chickenpox is a wild disease. If only periods could follow the same pattern.

Acting

So you're telling me I can fuck up my job, continue to do it over and over again until I get it right, and once I eventually do what I'm supposed to, people will call my work masterful? Sign me up.

Funny business aside, Broadway performers are a thousand times more talented than screen actors.

Ratios

I'm a big fan of ratios. Whenever two things are being compared, a ratio should almost always be put in play. Two of my favorite types of ratios are nipple to boob ratios and aspect ratios.

Aspect ratios suck. Didn't I drop over a thousand bucks on a brand new widescreen so I could finally use the entire TV? How much wider are they trying to make my movies? Those black bars have to go.

Nipple to boob is a game changer. For dudes and for chicks. You can be smoking hot with a money face and body, but if that top slides off and you're rocking dinner plates, game over, no thanks. And by dinner plates, I mean unnaturally large areolas.

Few things are more disappointing than finding out the person you've been pleasuring yourself to isn't as attractive as you once thought. I had to use tears for lube as I watched Heather Graham's grade drop three points during "Boogie Nights." The forest downstairs didn't help either.

Smackers

I pray to god you're not a smacker. If you are, you may not know yet. I don't think any of them know.

What causes the irritating lip smack sound when some people talk? And why are the people that do it absolutely repulsive?

There are only two noises that get to me. One turns me on and one pisses me off. Without a doubt, this is the latter. This has to be something these people can hear, right? I'm not sure what needs to be done to make this go away, but it must be done immediately. I instantly hate you if you make a smacking sound while talking. Stop trying to make out with your words and talk like a normal, respectful individual.

PS, if you were wondering, the other sound is your parents having sex.

The Night Shower

People who shower at night instead of the morning are icky. How on earth can you think showering before bed is equivalent to showering in the morning an hour before you go to work? I don't know about you, but I get filthy when I sleep. I drool, fart, sweat, and simply reek when I get up in the morning.

If you're one of these people who claim they save time by showering at night, I urge you to reconsider. There's a reason why everyone at work hates you. Not only do you smell a day dirtier, but your shampoo and conditioner lost its strength around 4 a.m. Your hair's disgusting, your wenis stinks, and the dried-up crusty shit on your face couldn't be more noticeable.

At the very least, take a morning bath.

Saying You Know What a Person Is Talking About When You Have No Idea

I do this constantly, and I'm waiting for someone to test me one day. I have nightmares about an exchange like this:

Me: "Of course I saw that movie, it was awesome."

Ex-Friend: "I know, now tell me what happened."

Luckily, this never happens since the storyteller will nod and move right along without realizing you have no idea what they're talking about.

I can't even ballpark the amount of times I've never heard of the book, movie, or song the person was referencing. There are also many instances when I'm simply too dumb to follow the conversation. Current events are my downfall. Generally, I have no clue what's happening in the world, and that bites me in the ass from time to time.

"Sure, I know why those people are at Guantanamo Bay."

When really, all I know is it's some sort of U.S. internment camp, and I think the Jamaican bobsled team is there.

The Corporate World

Let's take a super quick break from funny.

My single greatest motivation for writing this book is my absolute hatred of everything related to the word "corporate." The corporate world blows dick. It ruins you. It drains every drop of originality and creativity you ever had. For five days a week, for 8-12 hours a day, you have to pretend to be someone else.

There are certainly people out there who thrive in this kind of environment, and that's great, but I'm not one of them. The last thing I want to do in life is walk into an office every day, sit at the same desk, stare at a computer screen for eight hours, and pretend to care about the shit I'm working on. Repeating this day in and day out for the next 40 years doesn't sound particularly appealing. Frankly, facing this reality scares the living shit out of me. Thank god for my co-workers. Seeing people who've lived through this environment for thirty years is a real eye opener. It's no wonder they're so miserable.

I've worked in business for seven years. I've worked for three companies in three different fields: tobacco, laundry, and roofing. Talk about captivating work. I've tried to convince myself that it was the industry. I figured if I got into sports or television, it would be completely different. But in the end, I knew it wouldn't matter. It's not the field. It's so much more.

It's going to bed at night knowing what tomorrow brings. It's setting that same alarm at the same time. It's hearing it in the morning. It's putting on dress pants and a dress shirt. It's walking to your car. It's driving down the same road. It's seeing the same billboards. It's recognizing other cars. It's hitting the same traffic at the same time. It's parking your car in the same spot. It's waiting for your computer to boot up. It's making that same cup of coffee. It's opening Outlook. It's looking at your calendar. It's going to the 10 a.m. status meeting. It's talking about your work like you care. It's making presentations for executives. It's counting down the minutes until lunch. It's eating the same thing every day. It's eating it with the same people. It's learning every function in Excel. It's learning every shortcut in PowerPoint. It's giving presentations. It's doing work you won't get credit for. It's making someone else more money. It's interacting with people like you're a robot. It's hearing people use the same business words over and over again. It's realizing you've started using them too. It's knowing you really don't care. It's knowing there are at least 500 other things you would rather be doing. It's not being able to do those things.

I'm probably the last person to take advice from, but I have learned a few things during my relatively short journey thus far. It's simple. Do something that allows you to be yourself. There's nothing worse than losing yourself to your career.

Rant over. Let's make fun of everything again.

Skipped Poops

I can never poop if I'm out of my element. If I go away for the weekend, I'm not pooping. I can sit down and try, but nothing's coming out. I went away for summer camp once when I was twelve. I didn't poop. I was away for a week. That can't be normal.

Needless to say, my bathroom is not a place you want to be when I get home. As soon as I get back, I immediately make up for however many non-pooping days have accumulated. If I'm gone for a week, I'm spreading seven poops out over the next 12 hours.

I surprise myself sometimes. It's kind of crazy how much poo your body can hold when it comes down to it.

The Best Music Video of All Time

Jesse and the Rippers: Forever. Fat Fish Music.

Please YouTube this immediately. This is easily the single greatest music video ever made. You could've just been run over by a garbage truck, but this video will instantly make you feel like a million bucks. After you watch it in full, make sure you go back and carefully re-watch the magic at the 01:58 mark. If that's not the happiest man you've ever seen, you must know some seriously joyful people.

The next best part occurs shortly after. Not only is Uncle Jesse topless, he's holding his baby (Nikki), and there's no debate on the gender.

Rebecca was obviously a lucky lady.

Talking While Calling Someone

Doesn't it bother you when someone who calls is talking to someone else when you pick up and say hello? It's like they're surprised to hear someone on the other end.

When you call someone, focus on the person you're calling. Don't start a conversation with someone else if you're mid-dial. And don't come on and say "Hello?" like you had no idea I would be answering your call to begin with. You're the one calling me. I get to say "Hello" in the form of a question, not you.

Graffiti

If graffiti artists put as much effort into something that actually mattered, there's a good chance this world would be at least 15% more productive.

How do they graffiti some of these things? It blows me away when I'm on a highway and see "PLAYA4E" written on the face of a bridge. Sure it's in the stupidest font and color I've ever seen, but it's somehow painted onto a highway overpass.

The amount of effort that must go into graffitiing seems overwhelmingly unnecessary. No one cares that you snuck out in the middle of the night, closed down a highway, rented a fire truck, strapped a miner's flashlight to your head, used at least 173 cans of spray paint, wrote a useless word in a font no one can read, and had snacks and beverages on hand because it must have taken at least six hours. That kind of effort should lead to something epic. Instead, you leave normal people all over wondering what the fuck "TRIK" means.

Stop. Do something useful.

Entering a Vehicle

A simple "go ahead" would save you countless hours over a lifetime of thinking your car is broken after the jackass you're driving around decided it would be a good idea to pull the door handle as you simultaneously double-clicked the unlock button on your keyless entry.

Stop jumping the gun. From here on out, wait for the magic words.

People Don't Work

I'm convinced very few people actually work. When I go out for lunch, I see middle-aged couples playing tennis in the park. When I go to the mall, I see a thousand 23-45 year olds wearing tear-away track pants and sweatshirts. When I walk down the street, I see a mom and her ten-year-old son at 12:15 in the afternoon. Shouldn't she be at work? Shouldn't her kid be at school? Shouldn't these people have to be miserable for the majority of their lives like everyone else? I cherish playing tennis. I cherish going to the mall. The entire reason why these activities are so enjoyable is because they can only be done on a Saturday or Sunday. I can't play doubles at 1:30 on a Tuesday afternoon.

What am I doing wrong? Have these people finally figured it out? Can the system really be beat? Sure, people are unemployed, have vacation days, and work nights, but let's be real. There's no way in hell this many people fall into one of these categories.

I'm sick and tired of seeing so many people living the dream that I rarely leave my house if I have the day off. Let's just say I've been playing the peanut butter game with my dog a little too often these days.

Makeup

Makeup is the best and worst thing ever invented. It gives anyone the power to look temporarily acceptable. You can cover up some nasty shit with makeup. Pimples, warts, herpes, freckles, and birthmarks are just some of the repulsive things that people mask with this magical substance.

During a recent label-read, I realized there's some pretty disturbing stuff in makeup. The anal pouches of civet cats are just one of the many awesome ingredients. I don't know what a civet cat is, but an anal pouch belonging to anything doesn't sound pretty. I'm guessing this is why the majority of makeup is brown.

As a very average-looking male, I get offended by makeup. I always wondered, what would happen if dudes had a makeup-like tool available to them?

If an ugly girl puts on makeup before going to a bar and wants to be fucked, there's a ninety-five percent chance she'll get railed. If a disgusting non-makeup dude throws on a button-down before going to a bar and wants to be fucked, there's a two percent chance he'll get railed. Now, imagine if this same dude was allowed to rub anal pouches all over his face. He's a lot more fuckable now, isn't he?

Yanking Your Yo-Yo

Have you ever felt a little disappointed after touching yourself? It always seems like such a great idea during some down time, but comparing the burden of setup and cleanup versus the end result has become a significant struggle for me.

You're sitting on your couch, alone as usual with nothing to do, and the Shake Weight commercial comes on. As soon as the hot 35-year-old blonde in the green tank starts thrusting her arms back and forth, you immediately remember you can be doing this to yourself. You ponder your choices and are torn between unloading two days' worth of inventory or staying put as is. Ultimately, the answer is always, "Sure, what the hell,"

Grab your tissues, choice of lubricant (if you're not a dry hander), and your multimedia source of pleasure. Whether it's Good Housekeeping, a video, or a no-material-eyes-closed daydream jerk, you know the routine.

How long are you supposed to do it for? I'm never sure, so sometimes I stop myself from time to time if I think it's embarrassing how quickly I'd be able to finish.

Watch it fly, clean up, wipe off the rug, pee out the remains, clear your history, and get back on the couch.

Sometimes, not always, but sometimes... It's a little disappointing, isn't it?

Maybe it's because the more experienced you are, the more uneventful it gets. Maybe I'll throw a pinky in my butt next time out. Who knows?

NASA

Can we please stop building spaceships, probes, rovers, gigantic telescopes, and space stations? Like I said already, we're sitting on a mountain of debt, over $20 trillion to be exact. Don't you think it's time we wake up and realize there isn't life on Mars? Best case, we discover the remains of an organism that was alive 4.2 billion years ago. That'll save us.

I'm not a huge NASA fan. I'm all for photographing planets that are actually in our solar system, but besides that, spending money on anything else is entirely unnecessary.

Maybe I'm being too critical. Some of the work NASA's turned out has drastically impacted the lives of many:

Vast solar system found 127 light-years away

An enormous solar system of seven planets orbiting a sun-like star has been discovered 127 light-years from Earth. It is the largest planetary system ever to be discovered beyond the sun.

That's so close.

NASA warns solar flares from 'huge space storm' will cause devastation

Britain could face widespread power blackouts and be left without critical communication signals for long periods of time after the earth is hit by a once-in-a-generation "space storm," NASA has warned.

Right.

Most detailed pictures of Earth revealed by NASA

The most detailed and amazing set of composite satellite images of the Earth ever produced has been disclosed by NASA scientists.

Or, we could just open our eyes.

I'm looking forward to the next groundbreaking discovery.

Art

I used to hate abstract art because it's so dumb, but I've come to realize the "artists" who create abstract art are some of the most brilliant people out there. Over hundreds of years, they've duped people into thinking these kindergarten drawings are actually worth money. The fact that people think they can analyze a painting that looks like a circus rug is a joke.

Kazimir Malevich. Wikipedia this man immediately. I used to think Margaret Wise Brown and Laffit Pincay were my idols. That was before I stumbled across this mastermind. Kazimir was the pioneer of geometric abstract art. His lifelong masterpiece is called the "Black Square." Look it up. It's a black square. There may or may not be a tiny white dot in the middle, but that's pretty much it. Picture a blackboard with no chalk on it. Then pretend it's in the shape of a square instead of a rectangle. If you were alive 100 years ago and put this groundbreaking image onto a canvas, you would be an art legend.

Art is stupid.

Rich People

Why do rich people get all the free shit? The more money you have, the more stuff you get that you don't have to pay for. Makes sense.

Over half of all rich people did absolutely nothing on their own to achieve their financial status. These people are simply related to someone who spent their entire life working their ass off. I wouldn't complain if I walked into a boatload of money, but the fact that these morons can lollygag through life is complete bullcrap. They can't tell the difference between green and yellow, but they can certainly throw a potluck for their other pretentious douchebag friends.

Making money if you have money to begin with is a piece of cake. No matter what, you can always bank on interest. But there's a big difference between making three percent on five thousand dollars versus five million dollars. Instead of this accounting for only 150 bucks a year, these people are walking away with 150 grand. That's three times the average household income in the US. Income earned by people working 2,000 hours over the course of a year.

Franchising a restaurant is another simple way to make money. You don't have to do anything. The entire brand has been built for you. Don't worry about the menu, prices, or advertising. It's all taken care of. You just have to do whatever corporate says. I'd be swimming in it if I opened an In-N-Out Burger in NYC.

Real estate is another gold mine. According to TV, any two idiots can buy a rundown house for $100K, pay someone $50K to make it farm-themed, and sell it three months later for $300K.

It's depressing when you think about the people who have these opportunities simply because they're related to someone who's actually worked before. Paris Hilton is the classic example. If I presented her with an alligator, raccoon, and salamander, I'm not super sure she'd be able to label them correctly.

Gift Cards

Gift cards are a splendid gift idea. Let's face it: no one really cares what someone else wants, so as long as you can identify the correct category, the gift card is gold.

Deciding on the amount always trips me up, though. I recently gave my sister-in-law a $25 gift card to a shoe store. I'm such a dick. I gave her enough money to buy one shoe.

Use the gift card carefully. It already says you don't give a shit about the person, so at least make sure you give enough to cover the total cost of the present.

Be careful with significant others though. I gave my girlfriend a gift card to Chick-fil-A once and she didn't swallow for three months. I guess she still had a bad taste in her mouth because of their stance on homosexuals.

Rioting

Your team's a ten-point dog. There's 30 seconds left and they're up by three. You're feeling good. The winner takes the conference and is headed to the 'ship.

The other team's on the 40, going in. Field goal forces OT. TD wins it. It's third and five. The QB drops back and gets blindsided by your All-American defensive end. The ball pops out. Your fat DT sucks it up like it's a sprinkle falling from an ice cream cone.

The stadium erupts. Game over. Huge win.

I don't know about you, but my first thought is always, "Hey, now that we won, let's go fuck up everyone's shit. Let's burn and smash everything belonging to the people who were just rooting for the same team."

Rioting is silly.

The Itch

Do you ever get the inner butt itch that is just out of reach, but it kind of feels good, and you're in no rush for it to go away? I do, and I hate losing it.

Thunderstorms

A thunderstorm has the ability to change your emotions instantly. If you're at home, you immediately feel safe. If you're driving, you bask in the wonderment of the sights and sounds. If you're in a classroom or meeting, you're twenty times more likely to speak up, talk to the person next to you, or care way more than you did before witnessing the first bolt.

It's odd that a thunderstorm immediately creates a sense of togetherness and changes the attitude of a room. I don't know why it happens, and to be honest, I really don't care. I love it. As much of a pussy as that makes me sound, you know you love it, too.

I live for storms from the heavens. They're god's way of reminding Justin Bieber where he isn't going.

Handkerchiefs

First things first. Why is there a "D" in this word?

How nasty are handkerchiefs? The invention of the handkerchief, and the fact that it was taken seriously, perplexes me. What if you have to blow again and it's still wet and snotty? How do you know when it's time to wash it? How come everyone who uses them looks like they LARP on the weekends?

The handkerchief has very few things going for it. Eventually, there won't be any place left for the discharged snot to go. The fold-over method to keep snot inside the hanky will no longer be an option. Before you know it, there's bound to be snot to inside pocket contact.

You're better off using a cum rag. At least then you'll be moisturizing with protein.

The Mute Button

I have way too much faith in the mute button when I'm on conference calls at work. A simple slip, malfunction, or the slightest bit of forgetfulness can lead to someone overhearing me call the director a "taint".

The mute button can easily end a job or a relationship if the dipshit who's talking doesn't realize the button's pressed. A traditional phone user probably isn't familiar with the implications of poor mute button management, but if you've ever worked in an office for more than five minutes, you're well aware of the nonstop shit-talking that goes on.

"Are we on mute? Okay, good." This is a phrase you'll hear quite often as the imbecile in the Chicago office rambles on and on. All this means is someone on your end wants to make sure they're in the clear before they rip them apart.

The amount of shit-talking that occurs at work is astounding. I've heard a guy call a girl "loose" before.

We weren't on mute.

Richard

I feel for all the Richards out there.

I want to meet the guy who decided Dick would be the most suitable nickname for his buddy Richard. This guy sounds like someone I wouldn't mind spending some time with. It's so simple, yet so amazing. The fact that people took him seriously is awesome.

I have a friend named Rachel. Twat seems like the most appropriate nickname for her. Can this happen?

Amish

Amish people are complete hacks. I don't know how they've pulled off the "I'm such a good person because I don't use electricity" story for so long.

After dating a girl whose parents lived next door to the Amish, I had two epiphanies. The first was to break up with her immediately, because it was super weird. The second was realizing these people aren't all they're cracked up to be. The lifestyle claims they've become famous for are horseshit. And yes, horse is definitely the most appropriate word to precede the shit.

Not only are they consistently cruel to animals, they have phones, watch TV, and ride in cars. Here's the catch. As long as they don't personally own the electrically powered product or device they're using, they're good to go.

These bastards vacation by paying someone else to sin. Can they visit the Pyramids? Of course, all they have to do is buy a plane ticket. They don't own the plane, so it's perfectly acceptable for them to enjoy the in-flight movie while the airplane burns a few thousand gallons of gasoline.

Do they ever miss a playoff game or Super Bowl? Nope. They'll invite themselves over, steal the best seats on the couch, and not even bring the fucking queso you asked for. Hell, they'll even use your landline to call over the rest of their pilgrim friends. That's right. Every Amish family has a cell phone in their outhouse. As long as it isn't "convenient" to get to, it's fair game. It comes fully loaded with an unlimited data plan.

The stuff they watch on RedTube must be frightening.

Warehouses

Why are there so many abandoned warehouses and why is every window in every one of these places always shattered?

Let's tackle the quantity factor first. Warehouses seem like a pretty substantial investment. I'm not sure the best way to capitalize on these investments is to build one, use it for 5-10 years, and then decide you don't want to store things anymore. Whether it's a company or a group of private investors, whoever's responsible for the financial return of a warehouse is a complete shithead.

Blue-collar folk must get pretty livid when they find out their warehouse is shutting down, because the amount of damage and destruction done to these places is pretty incredible. I challenge you to find an abandoned warehouse with three windows fully intact. Rocks, bolts, belt sanders, and forklift legs are just some of the items Wally the warehouse worker must have used to break the windows on his last day.

Or, maybe he jumped.

Shit, that just got depressing.

Nincumpoop

That's right. I spell "nincumpoop" my own way. Any chance to throw "cum" into a word that already makes fun of someone is simply an added bonus.

Vomiting

The feeling immediately after vomiting is hands down the best five minutes in life. I've never felt better. I look forward to the sweaty forehead and uncontrollable mouth-watering because I'm on the verge of unleashing all of my pain and suffering into a toilet bowl.

Getting sick out of both ends is even more awesome. You may feel like you've been buried alive for 30 minutes out of the hour, but for those other 30 minutes—between six different bouts of vomit and diarrhea—life is good.

Even if you could bundle the feeling of a thousand hugs, I don't think it would compare to post-vomit. I don't think anything compares.

Pronunciation

Does anyone actually say it the second way?

Tomato/Tomato

Potato/Potato

See, you read both words the exact same way. The first way. The right way.

The Shirt Neck

There's no doubt the neck makes or breaks the shirt. Even if you have a perfectly fitting '02 Papa Roach world tour shirt, if the neck's off, game over. It's time to let Papa go.

Here are some of the most frequent shirt deal breakers:

1. Neck is stretched

2. Neck lining border fabric is too thick

3. Neck lining border fabric is too thin

4. Neck lining border fabric is a different color than the shirt itself

5. Neck is too high and too tight

6. Neck is too low and too loose

7. Neck is too wide and too shouldery

8. Neck is a V-neck

Could you imagine seeing the Rock in a baggy, stretched out tee? Talk about going from midnight to six.

Astronaut Food

Astronauts risk their lives takeoff after takeoff, travel through space at unreal speeds, hang out in floating space stations, and the best cuisine we can muster up for them are a few bags of dried-up ice cream? Come on. We build rockets that hoist large objects into space at 20,000 miles per hour, but we can't serve burgers on the Discovery 6?

Are microwaves frowned upon in space? How about charcoal grills? I see no reason why astronauts can't cozy up next to a fire pit after a long day's work. Is the risk really that high? They're decked out in the most flame-retardant costumes I've ever seen. I think an accidental ash on the floor would be OK.

The Butt Slap

The butt slap continues to grow in popularity and has spread outside the sports world, at least for me. I butt slap at work now. It's a job, right? Football players, basketball players, baseball players—they're all "working," right? So why can't I bring this joyous action into my own workplace?

If you keep your hand stiff and straight, it's completely asexual. The only way HR can get you is if you cup. Never cup.

If you're ever in a congratulatory situation but your target's backside is unreachable, just grab the person by the penis or pussy. That's OK now.

Divas

I never knew what this word meant or how it came to be. I always assumed it meant nothing more than a bitch, but I decided to let Wikipedia sort it out for me.

*A diva is a celebrated female singer. The term is used to describe a woman of outstanding talent in the world of opera, and, by extension, in **theatre**, cinema and popular music. The meaning of diva is closely related to that of "prima donna."*

The word "diva" is often used negatively, to describe a celebrity in film or music who is extremely demanding and fussy when it comes to personal privileges.

Sounds about right, but it looks like they spelled "theater" wrong. I'll jump on Wikipedia right now to correct this. By the way, if you're ever knee deep in Wikipedia and start seeing words whose only definition is "baby tomatoes," you're welcome. I went on an editing binge one night when I was blacked out.

Believe it or not, there's also a male term for diva:

*The male **divo** does exist in Italian and it is usually reserved for the most prominent leading tenors, like Enrico Caruso or Beniamino Gigli. The Italian term divismo describes the star-making system in the film industry.*

We need to use divo immediately.

Will Smith. Divo. Yanni. Divo. Julio Iglesias. Divo. Devon White. Divo.

Kevin Bacon. Divismo.

Leftovers

I don't know why I bother anymore. After struggling to finish another terrible bowl of sausage and quinoa, I wrap it up thinking I'll eat it a few days from now. Somewhere between six and twenty-seven days later, I'll find it, tear back the tin foil, inhale something akin to a moldy douche, and abruptly discard it.

I recently made a life changing no-leftover pledge to myself, minus a few exceptions:

1. Popcorn. Without a doubt, second day popcorn is the best "leftover" out there. I've started making bowls a day beforehand so I can toss it in the fridge overnight. Try it. It's splendid.

2. Lasagna. Most pasta is a no-go because the sauce gets too oily, but if you have a concentrated, clumped-together pasta dish like a lasagna or ziti, it's go time. Enjoy.

3. Cheese Doodles. Although not necessarily considered a leftover, an uncovered bowl of cheese doodles is unmistakable. Leave it out overnight and you'll be rewarded with the perfect blend of moisture and crunch. It's unreal.

4. Chinese. No reason needed.

5. Not pizza. I know. I'm a dick. But I'm sorry, leftover pizza is terrible. Maybe it's because I'm from the northeast where pizza's actually made right, but either way, second-day pizza is garbage. Especially if it's cold. Either throw it out or finish your pie the first time around you pansy.

Who Will Talk Next

I enjoy conversations with large groups of people. There's never any pressure and you don't have to worry about being put on the spot to pull random subject matter out of your ass. There's always someone else in the circle who's willing to keep the conversation going. It's comforting.

But what happens when the conversation eventually runs dry? What do you do if there's more than five seconds of silence? I'm not a big conversation revivalist, so I usually join others in the awkward "head down floor stare." Once you've run out of things to say for more than three seconds, time's up. Don't force it. However, I do enjoy seeing how long the awkwardness lasts before people go their separate ways.

If it were up to me, I'd say, "Well then, I'm not sure what else to talk about. It was nice. Thanks for the conversation." But no, society says we can't say the things we're actually feeling. We have to pretend to remain interested and force new topics which neither party actually cares anything about.

Dogs may be the clutchest things out there. They're a huge saving grace in the awkward conversation department. As soon as the conversation runs dry, the dog instantly becomes the center of attention. Someone will always make a crack about the dog's silly face, or ask a stupid question about its age in dog years.

This is why I love going to my uncle's house for family parties. Not only am I promised a worry-free night of continuous conversation, but I can pass gas at will. Either way, Dakota's got me covered.

Fake Names

I use Valentina at Panera and Gabriela at Blimpies. I'm just kidding about Blimpies. No one actually eats there.

The look of bewilderment while people write your name on the order is amazing. It's much more entertaining to wait for your food if the person behind the counter is debating whether or not you may be a Hispanic woman. What can they say? They can't question your name. That wouldn't be very polite. Instead, they'll spend the next five minutes trying to decide which part is between your legs.

Magicians

Magicians are enormously underused in society. Why don't we have as many magic clubs as comedy clubs? Who wouldn't want to sit down to a tasty dinner, throw back a few beers, and watch a magician pull baby doves out of his sock? It's a downright disgrace that the only place to find a magician is at a carnival or a five-year-olds birthday party.

For whatever reason, there are still non-believers out there who think magic is complete bullshit. I'm one of them, but I have no problem being temporarily mesmerized by a guy who can slice a human being in half. I know his hot side piece isn't actually cut in two, but I'll tell you what, I still have no idea how he does it.

Magicians are the true artists. They could spend their lives drawing pictures of circles and squares, but that'd be childish. Instead, they blow your mind.

Are sex magicians a thing? If not, they certainly should be. I'm still clueless when I'm staring at the curtains, so a little magic wouldn't hurt. In fact, I could see dudes getting together just like ladies do for fellatio classes. Similar to a girl showing you how to properly deep throat a banana, sex magicians could reveal tricks for pleasuring a vagina. But since there aren't any vagina-like fruits available to practice on, you'd have to rent prostitutes instead.

I've already envisioned my sex magician encounter, and it turns out to be a life-changing experience. He teaches me the "tickle." Middle finger up the A, thumb up the V. Once inserted, meet in the middle, feel your fingers touch, and tickle. My test prostitute simultaneously sneezes and squirts at the same time.

Stars and Oceans

Who are the geniuses profiting from the idiots who buy acres of ocean? Being able to sell something you do zero work for is my lifelong goal. If you're the first to claim a star on Orion's Belt, this somehow makes you the proprietary owner? How?

Fuck stars and oceans; I want to sell planets. Can you even fathom how much Saturn would go for on eBay? $3 billion easy. Consider this my ownership claim. In fact, I'll take all 8, including Earth. I'm only interested in real planets though, so no, I don't want Pluto. That dwarf's all yours.

If a bunch of jackasses can profit from selling the 5° 15' S 70° 58' E acre of Indian Ocean, then I should be able to make a decent buck if I want to sell Uranus. By the way, I'm still surprised Uranus hasn't been reclassified as a black hole yet.

Got 'em.

Bed Rest

The only reason why I would ever consider being a woman is for the possibility of bed rest during pregnancy. Do you realize how unbelievable this is? It can last anywhere from three days to three months, and you know what, I'm in.

The only potential rival to bed rest is hibernation. When you hibernate, you can't watch TV, but it is for a serious amount of time and once that alarm goes off, there's a good chance you'll wake up feeling better than post-vomit.

Nevertheless, in the end, bed rest may be shorter, but it's undeniably sweeter. The combination of unlimited food, drinks, and TV makes bed rest the clear cut favorite. Also, preparing for hibernation by spending two months digging for fruits and berries in near-freezing temps sounds awful.

Mall Kiosks

How stupid are these things? How many calendars can one person buy? Why is there a Verizon, AT&T, and Sprint kiosk fifteen feet from the actual store? And no, I don't want a bracelet that cures headaches.

This has to be rock bottom for a business owner. You sit on a wooden stool all day, talk to your one visiting friend, and watch aimlessly as another shopper walks by with no intention of even glancing in your direction.

If you're in the middle, you have no chance. You're like a sponsored link in a Google search. Have you ever clicked on one of those? I didn't think so. Sponsored links have no appeal, and a mall kiosk is the brick and mortar equivalent.

There's no doubt this space should be used for something else. I think it should be caged off and filled with the entire food chain from a rainforest. There's only one rule. The cage can't be maintained. Shit has to go down naturally. Young will be eaten, carcasses will rot, and cross-breeding will be rampant. People need to see the ruthless side of nature every once and a while. Is there a better place to showcase this to people than a mall?

Tater Tots

Why don't tater tots get more love? Very similar to the French fry, these splendid little balls of awesome are nearly impossible to find.

The French fry is good, but is it good enough that no other side should even be considered? There are at least two deep fryers in any fast-food restaurant, so why not fill one with French fries and the other with tater tots?

How did the potato arbitrarily become the go-to deep fried side dish that can accompany almost any meal? How did a vegetable become the worst thing in the world for you? Who could do such a thing?

Harry Dunne was right. The French are assholes.

Sharting

As of today, I've officially sharted twice in my life. In the scheme of things, I think two sharts before 30 is pretty damn good. My guess is I'd be somewhere in the 25th percentile.

My first shart happened in college. It was 2 p.m. on a lovely Sunday afternoon. It was after a relatively normal Saturday night: too many beers, too many shots, and too many slices of pizza. I'd been through the unlivable hangover before, but something was different this time. My morning farts were even wetter than usual. This particular one took about 10 seconds to push out, but I didn't think twice about forcing it through. There was no air release, no sound, no anything. It was just a hot pocket full of butt garbage. It kind of felt good. I enjoyed it for a minute or two before I snapped out of it and jumped in the shower to wash the feces off my leg. Being home was my only saving grace. I couldn't imagine sharting in public.

And then it happened. I was at work. It was 9:30 a.m. on a Tuesday. I was at my desk. I was in Excel. I just finished a nasty IF statement. IF statements get me excited. This time, a little too excited. I exploded.

I did the only thing I could. I clenched my cheeks, got up, and hobbled to the bathroom. I flew into the first vacant stall to assess the damage. It was everywhere. It was starting to penetrate through the micro holes in my boxers. I took off my drawers and pooped out the remains. I then wiped the excess poop from my dress pant crotch and wrapped my boxers up in TP. Once all other bathroom attendees finished up, I stormed out and disposed.

There was only one thing left to do. I had to freshen up. Naturally, I walked three floors down to the men's locker room, found an open locker, and ravaged through bags of gym clothes before locating a bottle of Axe. And there I was, ass-naked with a can of Phoenix in my hand, lathering my chode.

I was forced to free-ball the rest of the day. I don't know how porn stars do it. What if you forget to zip up after peeing? Walking out of the bathroom with my dick out is an all-time fear of mine.

I check my pants constantly these days. I let very few farts pass without the finger check. A quick finger down the pants can immediately determine disaster or triumph.

The 10

Finding an ATM that distributes cash in 10s is like finding one more fruit snack wedged in the corner of the wrapper. On top of that, it's strawberry.

Isn't it wonderful when you see $50 as an option for withdrawal? I'd pay an extra dollar surcharge per transaction if I could always walk away with a 10-dollar bill. I think 5's should be thrown into the mix as well. I anxiously look forward to the day when I can withdrawal 60 bucks in the form of two 20's, a 10, a 5, and five 1's.

It's nice to have options. Even though cash is now meaningless, the $10 machine is an unexpected treasure.

Kids Who Wear T-Shirts in the Pool

Why do parents feel the need to cover up their portly child's belly whenever they encounter a body of water?

Disgusting old fat dudes have no problem baring it all at the pool or beach, so why can't the next generation enjoy some sun? They're the furthest from self-conscious; they thrive on jolliness. Putting a t-shirt on a chubster only takes away from the self-degradation they feast on.

Let your kid live a little. I know full well it's not his choice that shirt's on.

Ranch

It baffles me that ranch is even considered a salad dressing. If ranch is in play, I see no reason why mayonnaise shouldn't be as well.

"I'll have the house salad please."

"What kind of dressing would you like with that?"

"Hmm, what do you have?"

"Italian, thousand island, oil and vinegar, raspberry vinaigrette, balsamic, and ranch."

"Oh, ranch, definitely ranch. Can I have some jalapeno poppers and potato chips with that as well? Thanks."

Ranch is on another level. Don't get me wrong—it's splendid, but I think we're pushing a few boundaries if we're considering it an ordinary dressing. It's certainly acceptable on pizza, vegetables, and chicken wings, but salad? It's a dipping sauce, plain and simple. If you regularly cover your salad in ranch, then there's a strong chance you wear a shirt in the pool.

I went through a serious ranch phase in college. Anything was in play. I once lathered a girl up in it before eating her out.

Her butt, of course.

Rubbernecking

The Driver's Ed program is a complete letdown. It's missing one crucial element. Before 15 and 16-year-olds even think about driving, they need to be exposed to every cause of rubbernecking. A five-hour video would do the trick. The first three hours should be dedicated to car crashes of all shapes and sizes. There should be close ups of glass, blood, bodies, police, stretchers, fire, fire trucks, ambulances, and whatever else has in one way or another been seen during an accident.

A solid hour of animal carcasses should follow. Footage of decapitated deer, rabbit, squirrel, elk, bear, opossum, and wolverine should get the point across. Besides, who doesn't love seeing a dead wolverine?

The next and final hour should be filled with police activity. The curriculum should be all encompassing and include everything from a routine traffic stop to a red neck towing his recently molested circus goat. If you were wondering, the goat's female and she strapped on. I'm OK if this portion gets pushed to the bonus features.

A five hour video would solve everything. A policeman handing out a broken taillight ticket to a Honda CRV will no longer be the most amazing thing you've ever seen in your life. Yes, it's a police car. Yes, his lights are flashing. Yes, the driver probably committed a minor violation. Yes, it's cool. But no, you don't have to go from sixty-five to five to look.

Have some class. Act like you've been there before.

Low Pressure Water Fountains

A water fountain has two responsibilities: be cold and be pressurized. Still, it doesn't seem like water fountain makers have figured it out yet. It's extremely disappointing when you stumble across a warm, unpressurized stream of water that barely trickles over the plastic spigot.

What's your move? Do you quench your thirst elsewhere, or go lip-on-spigot for that tasty sip of lukewarm water?

Regardless of stream length, there are people out there who use the same lip-on-spigot technique every time out. Fucking kids. They treat every water fountain like it's their mom's left tit. Which begs the question: how do some women get away with breastfeeding their toddler? Just because they're unhappy and are looking elsewhere for pleasure, I'm not entirely sure their four-year-old son should be brought into the mix.

Cows

"Hey hunny, look, all the cows are sitting down. That means we're in for a downpour," says the idiotic dad while driving his daughter home from ballet.

I'm sorry, but a cow doesn't know if it's going to rain. Cows sit down at least four or five times a day, so I'd like to see some figures correlating rainfall and sitting time.

Out of every US state, Texas has the most cows. I'm no paleontologist, but I have a hunch it doesn't even rain four times a day in Mawsynram, India, let alone a desolate place like Texas. And for the uneducated, Mawsynram, India is the wettest place on Earth.

Droughts must be extraordinarily tough on cows. I used to worry about a drought's impact on crops, but all along, I should've been more concerned about Pinky blowing out her left knee. Three months of non-stop standing can't be beneficial to a cow's key ligaments.

On a related note, just because the wind suddenly shifts from left to right doesn't mean god's about to pee on us. Seeing the back of a leaf isn't that unreasonable. It doesn't mean rain.

Stop telling your five-year-old daughter a storm's coming because cows get tired and the wind changes direction.

Fetishes

People with fetishes need to relax. There has to be a point in time when you realize you're just a complete weirdo, right?

My guess is all fetishes come into play when you're 35-40, single, and with a future as bright as a sepia colored crayon. This is when most middle-aged men find themselves scouring RedTube for anything with feet. Why is everyone so gung ho about the toe? My big toe looks like it was cummed on, thrown up on, and bled on at the same time. If someone comes within six inches of it, I'm pretty sure they're walking away with pink eye.

I wouldn't mind getting a foot job, though. Getting pleasured by the bottom of someone else's feet that haven't been sanitized in years does sound pretty appealing.

That definitely isn't why I have a cyst on my wiener.

Seasonal Things

I live for the seasons. Just thinking about seasonal foods and drinks has the ability to transport you back to an exact moment when they were enjoyed. These should conjure up a few arousing feelings for you:

- Winter
  - Hot Cocoa
  - Hot Cider
  - Peanut Butter Balls
  - Candy Canes
  - Graham Crackers
  - Eggnog
- Spring
  - Cheese and Crackers
  - Pasta Salad
  - Greens
  - Garlic
  - Asparagus

- o Easter Ham
- o Strawberry Pie
- o Sun Showers
- Summer
  - o Ice Pops
  - o Funnel Cake
  - o Watermelon
  - o Burgers and Dogs
  - o Potato Salad
  - o Lemonade
  - o Iced Tea
  - o Fresh Corn
  - o Tomatoes
  - o Strawberries
- Fall
  - o Pumpkin Pie
  - o Pumpkin Bread
  - o Pumpkin Ale

- o   Anything Pumpkin

- o   Apple Cider

- o   Acorn Squash

- o   Mac and Cheese

- o   Cinnamon Cookies

- o   Chili

- o   Sweet Potatoes

I'm a sucker for anything seasonal. I spend 25% of my income at Yankee Candle so my house can smell like early morning dew after a starry night in a rolling meadow during the month of April.

Spring's the best because that's when asparagus is the ripest and most potent. Have you ever peed on anyone after eating it? I highly recommend it if you're looking for a good prank to pull around the dorm or office. The stank is nearly impossible to get out.

Going Potty Outside the Potty

Peeing in a pool or shower is completely acceptable and should always be encouraged. I feel sorry for you if you leave a body of water every time the tinkle ferry calls.

Pools are standard fare. Slowly disengage from your friends, pretend your checking out how deep the deep end is, and let it ride. If you're with close friends, let them know where the damage was done. It typically takes 90 seconds for pee to clear out.

If you're not in a position to announce your triumph, my only advice is keep talking. There are too many times when people wander off and completely shut down. Don't give yourself up so easily. Always stay engaged while urinating. No one will think twice about it until you're still in the pool after five hours, have crushed 8-10 beers, and haven't been within five feet of the stairs.

Peeing in the shower is very private and very fun. Although there's a potty one foot from where you are, it should never be used if you're about to shower—especially if you're a woman. Peeing while standing up is a beautiful thing. Make sure to spray it all over your ankles and feet. It's good for the toes.

———

The ocean opens up a whole world of opportunity. Peeing is a given, but pooping is in play as well if each of these conditions are met:

1. You're in up to your nipples

2. There is a mild to non-existent undertow

3. There is no one within a five yard radius

4. You're all the way to the left or right side of the lifeguard zone

    a. Depends on the current. For example, if the current is going right to left, you should be on the left side of the zone, ensuring all poop floats away from fellow swimmers

5. You spread your cheeks for a clean release

6. You wait 15 minutes before coming on shore

7. You security wipe within the hour

8. You get a tetanus shot within a week

Pooping in the ocean is like masturbating in public. You know it's not socially acceptable, but as soon as you do it once, you're all in. There's no chance you're leaving the beach again.

Closing Thoughts

Well, that's it for now. I know. I'm right there with you. "Thank god. Please shut the fuck up."

It may take a few months for this book to change the world, but in the meanwhile, do your part. Call people out, make fun of everything, make fun of yourself, make serious situations not so serious, say something that shouldn't be said, and always wear a seatbelt.

While we certainly covered a lot of ground, there are still a million other things out there to make fun of. Take it from here.

After all, life is funny.

About the Author

Age 0: My first poop

Age 1: My first word: "come"

Age 2: The first time I threw up in my mouth

Age 3: Living the dream: up and running, still no school

Age 4: My first and last theft: a Hershey's bar from Walgreens

Age 5: Officially potty trained

Age 6: My first of many pinewood derby wins

Age 7: My first erection

Age 8: Disney World

Age 9: I fill five pillow cases with candy, my biggest Halloween haul ever recorded

Age 10: My first boobs: Kate Winslet in Titanic

Age 11: Britney and Christina (the hot 18 year-old versions)

Age 12: My infamous no-poop-for-a-week camping trip

Age 13: I realize I'm not the only one with a small penis after seeing the "David" statue

Age 14: My eighth consecutive little league all-star appearance

Age 15: My first wet dream

Age 16: The first time a period ruined everything

Age 17: Caught muff diving in the woods

Age 18: My last bath with Dad

Age 19: My pedophile 'stache

Age 20: I switch teams for a night

Age 21: My first and last Somalian

Age 22: The day I realize real life blows

Age 23: My first cum swap

Age 24: My first rim job on the receiving end

Age 25: The royal wedding

Age 26: Home Depot and Bed Bath and Beyond

Age 27: My last bed wet

Age 28: My third shart?

My Favorites:

- Color: Cornflower Blue
- Animal: Bigfoot
- Amphibian: Newt
- Number: 9
- Cereal: Cinnamon Toast Crunch
- Fruit Snack: Gushers
- Dipping Snack: Dunkaroos
- Apple: Honey Crisp
- Root Beer: Stewart's
- Pen Color: Blue
- Internet Site: Dogpile.com
- Dinosaur: Dilophosaurus
- Tree: Oak
- Cloud: Stratus
- Soap: Dial Bars
- Sport: Football
- "Sport": Badminton or Curling

- Wrestler: Val Venis

- Video Game: Streets of Rage 2

- Book: The Kid Who Only Hit Homers

- Season: Summer

- Food: Penne a la Vodka

- Instrument: Oboe

- Gatorade: Orange

- Gum: Big League Chew

- Ingredient: Garlic

- TV Show: Saved by the Bell

- TV Character: Albert Clifford Slater

- Movie: D2

- Movie Character: Chet Stedman

- Inventor: John Landis Mason

- Ninja Turtle: Leonardo

- Porn: Beastiality

- Screw Driver: Phillips Head

- State: South Dakota

- Ocean: Southern

- Holiday: Memorial Day

- Band: Zack Attack

- Song: Friends Forever

- Author: RL Stine

- Body Part: Lobes

- Coat Style: Military

- Juice: Apple

- Vagina Size: 2

If you'd like to drop me a note, send words of wisdom, or make fun of me, hit me up at seven.munson@gmail.com.